Advance Praise for Thistles & Thorns

"In a world where tragedy looms and grief is inevitable, we must all find a way to thrive. In her heartfelt true crime memoir, *Thistles & Thorns*, Jessica Lee Peterson shares her dark tale of living with a dangerous, narcissistic man and the courage and strength it takes to move on after her entire life is shattered. A true survivor's story that you will not forget. Well worth the read!"

—Edward S. Scott,
Author of *Dark Daze & Foggy Nights*
and Detective of Ashwaubenon Public Safety, Retired

"Jessica Lee Peterson tells a heartbreaking story of unimaginable shock and unthinkable grief after her three children are murdered by their father. A story of survival with unseen wounds that never heal."

—C. C. Harrison,
Award-winning Mystery Author of *Death by G-String:
A Coyote Canyon Ladies Ukulele Club Mystery*

"How does someone recover from the unthinkable? One heartbreaking, unflinchingly humane answer mourns and defiantly lives within these pages. Jessica bravely and honestly shares the horror and hope of going on."

—Paul Tremblay,
Author of *A Head Full of Ghosts*

"I give Jessica Lee Peterson a huge amount of credit for sharing some very private moments with the world in her book, *Thistles & Thorns*. It takes a strong person and a bonded family to share about some of those harder moments. Jessica is an incredibly strong woman and I am in awe of her ability to dig deep and find the drive to move forward."

—Billi Jo Baneck,
Brown County, Wisconsin 911 Dispatcher Supervisor

"*Thistles & Thorns* by Jessica Lee Peterson is a gut-wrenching true crime story of the horrendous murders of three beautiful little girls. Her girls. But, the book goes beyond these murders, delving into how a mother can survive such a catastrophe and maintain her faith in her fellow humans. This is a must read, for not only true crime fans, but readers seeking to renew their faith in humankind, as well as a testament to a mother's resilience."

—Steve Daniels,
High-Risk Parole Agent, Retired, and True Crime Author

"*Thistles and Thorns* recalls the tragic events of Jessica Lee Peterson's life in the most uplifting way. She reminded me that even in the face of grief, we can heal, survive, and continue living."

—Jeanne Gruehn,
Brown Deer Police Officer, Retired

"Jessica Lee Peterson's story is an intimate and raw look into her life as a mother. It is a collage of sharp fragments and soft pieces, threaded together by a mother's eternal love and commitment to her children. Jessica beautifully weaves a tapestry of memories, interchanging fibers of warmth and humor with loss and grief. Avoid the temptation to pretend the book is fiction, you will come to love Jessica and her girls too much to cheat them of this. Let the words seep into your bones and allow your heart to swell even in knowing it will inevitably create more shards as it shatters; as a mother does, Jessica will stitch the pieces together again, though never in the same way that it was. *Thistles & Thorns* is a testament to the healing power of community and a reminder that there is life beyond grief if we dare to keep living."

—Callie Trautmiller, Award-winning Author of *Becoming American*

Thistles & Thorns

JESSICA LEE PETERSON

Thistles & Thorns

JESSICA LEE PETERSON

Written Dreams Publishing

Publisher/Executive Editor: Brittiany Koren
Copy-editor: Melinda Peterson
Cover Art Designer: Ed Vincent/ENC Graphics
Interior Layout Designer: Amit Dey
Ebook Layout Designer: Amit Dey

Category: True Crime Memoir
Description: The true story of one mother's grief, hope, and love for her three young daughters after their brutal murders.
Hard Cover ISBN: 978-1-951375-76-8
Paperback ISBN: 978-1-951375-77-5
Ebook ISBN: 978-1-951375-78-2
LOC Catalogue Data: Applied for.

First Edition published by Written Dreams Publishing in October, 2022.
Ebook Edition published by Written Dreams Publishing in October, 2022.

Green Bay, Wisconsin
Printed in the United States of America.

To those I lost and those who keep me tethered.
I love you all.

Dear Brave Reader,

I commend you for embarking on this journey with me. Writing is a vulnerable act of exposure and so is reading. You start a book, but you never know where it will take you. My tale is not for the faint of heart and I applaud you for willingly walking this path with me. There are many things in this life that make hard things more bearable. Love, food, and music are a few for me. Music especially, has saved me more times than I can recall. That is why I chose to use song titles for my chapters and put together a playlist for you. I hope that the music and my story pull you into the depths and carry you back to the light again.

Best Intentions,
Jessica Lee Peterson

Thistles & Thorns Play List

"Sleeping Sickness" by City and Colour
"I Don't Wanna Grow Up" by Tom Waits
"Untouchable Face" by Ani DiFranco
"Brown Eyed Girl" by Van Morrison
"Float On" by Modest Mouse
"Video Games" by Lana Del Rey
"We're Going to Be Friends" by The White Stripes
"Cecilia" by Simon & Garfunkel
"Mama, I'm Coming Home" by Ozzy Osbourne
"Kiss With A Fist" by Florence + The Machine
"Black Cadillacs" by Modest Mouse
"Kiss Me Again" by Jessica Lea Mayfield
"Going Out In Style" by Dropkick Murphy's
"Holland, 1945" by Neutral Milk Hotel
"this is me trying" by Taylor Swift
"The Field" by Mason Jennings
"You Were Born" by Cloud Cult
"Only Son of the Ladiesman" by Father John Misty
"Stubborn Love" by The Lumineers

Prologue

Sleeping Sickness

Many people know the basics of how my world ended on July 10th, 2012, but few know the whole story of how I lost my girls way too soon...

Where to begin. With a punch in the face? A poorly-timed positive pregnancy test? The phone call that brought me to my knees? The 100th morning when I woke up and had to remember again that I was no longer a mother? Or the moment when I knew I'd survived, whether I wanted to or not?

For the sake of my own sanity, I'll start with me and my last moments with my girls: Amara Rose, age eleven going on seventy. Sophie Marie, an established artist after eight orbits around the sun. And baby Cecilia Lee—Cea, who'd ruled the roost since her arrival five years earlier. And then there was me, or at least who I used to be when I stood on the other side of tragedy. Jessica Lee, am—was—will always be their mother.

It was a chaotic morning like most. We all had dentist appointments early in the day. Amara and Sophie both had sealant put on their teeth that day because they had grown-up teeth worthy of extra protection, while Cea still hadn't lost a single tooth. The girls loved visiting our dentist, while I've always loathed it. The combination of the uncomfortable sensation of having someone root around in your mouth and because I think teeth are creepy.

Cea didn't think that, though. She died without ever knowing the magic of having a fairy sneak into her room to trade a tooth for a silver dollar coin.

I still have Amara's and Sophie's baby teeth in a little box on my bookshelf. I never knew what to do with their teeth after I put my tooth fairy wings away. I keep a note in the box that Amara once left for the tooth fairy.

Dear tooth Fairy,

may I pleas have a photo. Not drawn. thank you.

Amara

Sophie once busted me and asked why I had a box full of teeth hidden in my room. I panicked and prioritized salvaging magic over maintaining my reputation as a sane mother.

"Those are the trophies I keep from all the little kids who've snooped in my room," I said with the most sinister face I could muster.

She quirked her eyebrow at me and smirked. "I am going to call the police and tell them you've been taking kids' teeth," she said.

I took a long sip of coffee and gave her a look. "If the police come and investigate me," I said, "they'll look into your business, too."

Sophie thought a bit too long for my comfort and said "nevermind" before scooting out of the kitchen to go bury some evidence.

Amara had band camp that morning, so she was first in the dentist's chair. I watched her lead the hygienist back to the exam room, chatting about starting middle school and her plans for the rest of the summer. I hung out in the waiting room with the younger two girls, sending each one off as their names were called.

Our nanny Dealla picked Amara up and dropped her off at school for band camp, then came back for the other two. I don't remember if I even hugged them good-bye. It was the normal rush of rotating bodies and signing paperwork. Why stop the rushing river of responsibilities to hold my babies and tell them I loved them when I expected decades of hugs, kisses, and opportunities to luxuriate in their presence?

I finished my appointment, made a half-hearted promise to floss more often, and headed into work to fix the world one care conference at a time.

While at work, I couldn't stop thinking about what was coming. We had big plans that night. I was going to introduce the girls to Matthew, the man with whom I'd become quite smitten with over the previous few weeks. Cooking for people is my primary love language and that night I planned on making a classic pasta feast. After dinner, we were attending a concert in the park to see a local band, Caroline Smith and the Good Night Sleeps.

The night before we'd practiced hula-hooping while listening to the band's song "Tank Top." Amara had become quite competitive in the hula-hooping arena and was getting a bit too close to my own crown for comfort. Later, after they were all sound asleep, Matt came over to further feed my infatuation with him. Walking past their bedroom doors, behind which they dreamed their last dreams, was the closest he'd ever get to meeting them.

The day progressed, and that afternoon while I was still at work, Blake, the girls' father, called. I was in the middle of writing case notes about my attempts to get an elderly client to accept in-home services, and I was irritated with having to deal with him yet again. Blake hadn't seen the girls in almost three months. We had been spending the last month trying to repair his relationships with the girls and I via Skype and stilted phone calls. He was supposed to be in North Dakota cashing in on the building boom, a reaction to the oil boom, but instead he was in town to see the girls.

"What do you mean you're here in the cities?" I asked, my attention on data entry.

"I had to drive one of the vans down to get it fixed at headquarters and my train back doesn't leave until late tonight," he smoothly poured his lie into my ear. "Jess, I thought I could come over and see you and the girls."

"We have plans tonight," I snapped. "You can't just pop in to town and expect us to drop everything. It's not fair to the kids."

"What are they doing right now?" he asked.

"They are with Dealla at the house," I said. "I suppose you could go to the house and see them for a little bit. But I want you gone before I get home at five."

He filled in a few logistical worries, saying he could borrow a car and that he'd be gone before my date night, even though I hadn't mentioned Matt coming over.

Who was I to deny my children the attention of their wayward father? I thought he was trying to be better. I called Dealla to tell her about the change in plans and gave her my blessing to leave as soon as he got there.

I spoke briefly to Amara on the phone at the same time, but can't recall the details of her words or the sound of her voice.

Though, I remember asking her a question. "Honey, are you okay with having him popping in like this?"

She'd struggled more than the other two girls with his vanishing acts. But she reassured me in her typical pre-teen manner with a firm tone that brushed up against condescending.

"Mom, I can handle it," she said. "Sophie and Cea really want to see him."

She wasn't wrong. I know for certain that all three were ecstatic to show Blake all their projects and the treasures they'd accumulated since the last time they saw him. I released a sigh of frustration that my big girl was being played like a yo-yo by her dad.

"Call me if you need me, love. I am just doing paperwork." We ended the call how we ended all calls with our simultaneous "Love you, bye."

I finished my workday and left the building. As I was walking to my car, to a future that only seemed brighter with every step I took, my cell phone rang. It was Blake again. I answered.

"You can come home now," he said. "I've killed the kids."

My knees buckled and I grabbed the car door to stop from hitting the pavement. I curled up like I'd been punched in the gut.

"That isn't funny!" I screamed into the phone. "You can't make jokes like that. Stop lying!"

But he'd already hung up, so my pleas echoed into the dead air.

Having the training I did as a social worker, my first full thought was, "Someone needs to get there *now*."

I scrambled into my car and called 9-1-1 as I buckled up. I desperately hoped the girls were still alive and Blake was bluffing, but I called the police as a precaution. I did not trust Blake at all. I didn't trust him to tell me the truth, but I also didn't trust him to lie to me about the one thing I wanted so badly to be false. I needed to believe he was just trying to terrorize me, torturing me. It was a true juxtaposition of both knowing his words were the truth and refusing to acknowledge a world where they would be. I was reduced to a motive that someone had to get to my babies immediately. After that, I was on autopilot.

I drove straight to the police station, but the following hours, days, weeks, and even months ahead are still riddled with ragged holes where recollection should be. I sat in a conference room in a tornado of numbness for an eternity until an officer broke through the howling winds of my fear. He confirmed my beautiful daughters were dead. Blake hadn't lied. As much as I wanted it to be untrue, willed it to be a bad dream, it was the awful truth.

My story is tattered and has missing pieces, just like my heart. It is surreal and nonsensical, just like my reality. I won't lie. It hurts deeply.

I can't promise my story isn't free of inaccuracies. I thought about donning an investigator's hat and getting the full scoop by interrogating every witness to fill in those gaps, maybe scouring the online archives for media reports, or requesting the evidence in the trial. I could still, but I won't, because it wouldn't be *my* story.

My memory from those hard days come in spurts, flashes if you will. It is the only explanation I know of how things happened. Enough excuses. Here we go...

xviii   *Thistles & Thorns*

Flash: I'm in a conference room. I've been here before. It's where I wrote my statement about threats Blake was making toward me months ago. Dawn, one of my oldest friends, is looking at me with the saddest eyes I've ever seen. Why is she here? Who has her kids? The girls, oh god... Now I remember...

Flash: My babies...my sweet little girls...are dead. Dear goddess, what is that awful sound? That keening. It's me! I'm making that noise and I can't stop. My arms are so empty. My heart is so empty. So so empty. How can emptiness feel this heavy? Not real not real not real not real.

Flash: I see a gun in a leather holster. It fills my entire view. I want that gun so badly I can taste it. It won't end my suffering.

Flash: Another room, one without windows. It feels small, claustrophobic. I hear a noise on the other side of the door. It's Blake. He is on the other side. Evil bastard. I'll tear him apart. Rage filled my brain. A priest, there to support me, is holding me back. I'm growling, straining to get through the door.

Flash: I'm on the phone. I hear the words echoing out of my mouth. "He killed the kids. Don't go to the house." Sorrow engulfs me.

Flash: I'm being asked about dismantled smoke detectors and gasoline spilled in the basement. I can see flames that were never lit.

Flash: I'm walking out of the police station. A smudge with a human shape speaks to me. "That guy you're dating," the smudge says. "He was here. You should give him a call."

Flash: I'm on a gurney in the emergency room. "Here's some Ativan," someone said to me. "It'll help."

"Can anything really help?" I ask them, or maybe I just thought it. Nothing helps. The devastation is too vast, and the pain simply will not be contained.

Flash: I'm in a hotel room. Matt is holding me. "Matt, oh Matt...why?" I'm crying. He's crying. My parents are there. I'm drowning in sorrow.

Waking up each day was so damn hard those first few weeks. First, there were the blissful seconds of forgetting the world had ended, followed quickly by the complete terror-filled disorientation of having no idea where I was. Then, it'd all come crashing in at once.

My children are dead.

I am no one's mother.

I have no purpose.

My home is a crime scene.

I am homeless.

My girls are gone, but they still need me.

I must *keep moving...*

As the days bled into weeks, my bouts of being fully present lengthened with each passing day. Eventually, I was able to resist the darkness more days than not. I'd get up and do the things that needed doing. I still had a lot to do. Amara, Sophie, and Cecilia were gone, and as much as I wanted to join them desperately, I couldn't. I could not further add to the hurt of those surrounding me.

Most of all, I wouldn't let that evil bastard get what he wanted. To destroy me. My survival would be a testament to my children, to spite that same darkness trying to consume me.

I was encircled by family and friends from every corner of the country. I was embraced by strangers and professionals. I was never alone. Seriously, my mother would barely let me piss in private. Somehow, despite the constant surveillance, or more likely because of it, I was able to dodge the media for a very long time. A big part of what made that possible was that I was now officially homeless.

I'd left my home early the morning of July 10th with every intention of returning. Dishes in the sink, dirty clothes in the hamper, an unmade bed. I had put on a purple and white plaid sundress that was cute but work appropriate. It was the last thing my girls ever saw me in, the last garment their hands touched.

I still have that dress. I never wear it, but I don't know what to do with it. As far as I can tell, its sole purpose is to randomly pop up in my closet occasionally and flood me with memories. Besides my keys and cell phone, it was all that I took from the house I never stepped foot in again.

It's one of those logistical things you don't ever think about. Why would you? When a triple homicide and attempted arson is perpetrated in the building that contains *all* of your worldly possessions, you don't get the chance to just go back in and grab your stuff.

The women in the victims advocates' office did their damnedest to get me some clean undies and other clothes from my bedroom, but those arguments were defeated by police protocol. Turns out, evidence is more essential than a grieving woman's need for essentials.

When they couldn't go themselves, they advocated that the police send in a female officer, but instead, the duty was given to a young man.

In my closet, I'd kept a laundry basket where I would toss stuff that the girls had outgrown or I'd grown tired of wearing. These cast-offs were meant to be donated when the pile got big enough. My guess is the male officer went into my bedroom with a bag in hand, maybe even a blindfold, and grabbed some random items before running from the horror show. So, when I opened up my loot on the hotel bed, one of the first things I spotted was some of Sophie's old, rejected clothes. Next up was a lacey thong snagged on a pair of wool work pants. Few items in the bag were useful.

At that time, having less was easier. I was moved around a lot at first, a different hotel in a different town almost every day. I remember one hotel more than the others. It was where we spent the most time, where my extended family entrenched themselves in the "war room" for meetings and organizing memorials. The hotel was where all the professionals would come to meet with the bereaved and those supporting us. For me, it wasn't just an easy place for the authorities and such to get as many of us in one spot at a time. This hotel was familiar and haunted.

The last time I'd visited that particular hotel was for Cea's fifth and final birthday party. Iris, one of my oldest and dearest friends, and her kids had come up for Mother's Day weekend, so I'd rented out the pool area to celebrate my baby's special day. Dawn and her children had also joined in for a wild time of cannon balls and diving contests. It was a day filled with laughter, and as usual, a little jealousy from siblings. No gift is quite as sweet as your sister's envy.

When I stayed there this time, it was much different. Whenever I had to travel down the hallway for another announcement from the medical examiner, or the police, or lawyers, or the mortician, the chlorine wafting down was a constant slap in the face of my new reality.

One afternoon, I wandered out the hotel's front door headed to who knows where, and for a horrid moment my protective fog abandoned me. There it was, the last place I saw my children alive. The hotel just so happened to be right next door to our dentist's office.

I crumpled.

Iris came running out to find me clawing my face, wailing in open-mouthed hiccupping sobs. She wrapped her arms around me as she shed her own tears, willing me not to fall apart. Her arms were replaced by a numbness, and eventually, I was able to sink back into a pit of quiet despair.

We walked back into the hotel, past that chlorine stench into my hotel room.

When I was an intolerable child, I'd go to the pool at the local high school where my sister, Olivia, was a lifeguard. I'd jump into the deep end and quickly sink to the bottom. I'd sit and stare at the forms moving above me on the surface. Top-side now and then, another lifeguard would sidle up to my sis.

"She's been down there a long time," they'd say.

Olivia would shrug. "She'll come up eventually. She always does."

Chapter One

I Don't Wanna Grow Up

My father named me Jessica Lee. I came into this world six weeks early, already defying my parents' expectations.

From that day, I've been a contradiction. The youngest in my family but the oldest soul. I spent my childhood either buried in a book or running wild in the woods. I was as comfortable on the farm as I was in the city. As a teenager, I rebelled and conformed to equal extremes, consistently responsible and reliably wild. I found my tribe among the skateboarders and outcasts, but my closest friends were from advanced placement classes. While I loved to party on the rough side of town, I knew the college track was my ticket to freedom.

That's how I found myself 500 miles away from my friends and family in the fall of 1999. I was twenty years old, and I'd just transferred to Minnesota State University for my junior year, working toward a degree in social work.

Minnesota was the sixth state I called home, MNSU the fifth school I attended. My dad had been a traveling salesman, so I'd lived in three different states before turning three. When I was a toddler, my parents bought a farm equipment business in rural Pennsylvania. They poured their lives into that company, and after a decade of struggles, it finally failed. My family broke apart for a year after that, and when the smoke cleared, I was living in a new place surrounded by strangers. So, by the time I moved to Minnesota, I was used to being the new kid in town. This time, though, I needed a job. Luckily, I'd had plenty of experience.

When I was ten years old, I started to get babysitting gigs. At thirteen, I lived with my older sister in South Dakota for a summer and earned my first real paycheck cleaning hotel rooms at the Super 8. I branched out into the food industry and did every job from washing dishes to serving filet mignon. I'd done my share of farm work, housework, and office work. My resume in 1999 was such that I barely had to *try* to get a coveted job slinging coffee to students at the University Campus café.

I was behind the bar cleaning the espresso machine when Blake walked in. (He would eventually murder my children.)

Like any good barista, I had a solid feel for the clientele, and I was sure I'd never seen him before. He looked like a Greek statue brought to life with thick, curly brown hair, a large Roman nose, and striking blue eyes. He was tall, and I could tell he was muscular under his plain shirt and relaxed jeans.

He stared at the menu for two clicks too long, so I looked at him and said, "Any day now. I have better things to do, you know, like scratching my ass."

He was impressed with my spiked bleach blonde hair, Doc Marten boots, and caustically sarcastic wit. He asked if I had any recommendations, so I said, "The Better than Sex latte is popular, but I can't say it's actually better than sex." I gave him a once-over and added, "But maybe it's better than the sex you're having."

He cracked that grin that'd do me in, and said, "You can only do so much yourself."

After that, he started coming in every day for my shift, sitting at the bar pretending to study. Early November crept into Thanksgiving, and I got to know Blake better.

He was a twenty-two-year-old freshman who'd been born and raised in the Twin Cities. He was the second of four sons born within five years.

His mother was an ardent Catholic who strived to raise the boys to be devout followers, but Blake denounced the church as soon as he could.

He got into trouble at a young age. His crimes tended to be financially motivated, from shoplifting to stealing from neighbors. When he was a teenager, he stole a gun from a family friend and took it to school to sell it. He was expelled for that one.

His mother ended up leaving. She moved away around the time he graduated from high school. His father treated the boys like roommates. Blake's tendency to do what he wanted got him kicked out of the house shortly before he decided to give college a shot. He'd spent a few years working as a framer for a home construction company and went to college after working in some pretty miserable conditions. He chose the University of Minnesota at Mankato because his baby brother, whom he'd always been closest to, was headed there in the fall.

Once, during one of our many moves much later, I found a list he'd written for reasons to go to college. The second item was: "To find a wife."

Whenever Blake and I would talk, I kept forgetting to mention my boyfriend.

Aden, my first real serious boyfriend, was attending Gustavus Adolphus College in St. Peter, just 15 miles away, for his freshman year. Aden and I had gone to the same high school, and we started dating the summer after my freshman year of college. He was a year younger than me and had an idyllic yet simple upbringing. Mine had been a little more complicated and challenging. These differences brought us together at first—I craved the comfort his stable life offered, he liked the novelty of my varied experiences—but these differences soon started to chafe. I wanted someone to relate to my jaded worldviews, he needed someone to join him in the excitement of being on the cusp of adulthood.

We hadn't gotten to the official break-up point yet. So, like any girl who's monogamous by nature and faced with a temptation to stray, I attempted to eliminate the threat: I tried to set Blake up with one of my closest girlfriends, Quinn.

She was a passionate feminist with a hippy flavor. We'd met in a social work class, where she'd taken one look at my pleather pants and spiked dog collar and offered up the open seat next to her. When she told me she was a vegetarian, I said, "Vegetarians are just glorified picky eaters." To this day, I still bitch about being forced to accommodate her limited diet whenever I cook her dinner.

The plan to set Quinn and Blake up went like this: I'd throw a college house party to celebrate my first adult furniture purchase—a cheap table from a local big box store. There'd be lots of people, plenty of drinking, loud music, and dancing. Blake had told me that he was spending a lot of time playing computer games alone in his dorm room, so I was sure if he got some exposure to other girls he wouldn't find me as alluring. Quinn was dynamic and challenging. She used her earthy style to cover her beauty, but it would show through despite all her efforts. I felt that out of all of my friends she was the most likely to attract Blake's attention. So, I introduced the two of them, plied them with alcohol, and gave them some space. I headed back to the makeshift bar for another drink and to gossip with the other partiers about whether or not my matchmaking would be successful.

When I finally made it back, they were vehemently arguing, not a drop of attraction to be sensed in either direction. Quinn later said it was obvious he was only interested in me and she didn't feel like wasting her time. In any case, he'd said something during their time together that set her off.

While there, I heard Blake say, "You're not a feminist, you just hate men." He followed it with a suggestion to "take that pent-up rage and let it out." As such, we all lined up to punch him.

Keep in mind, it was 1999, and *Fight Club* had just been released. It was one of the most innovative movies I had ever seen, and it introduced a whole new style of anarchy for the offspring of the counterculture generation. If you've never seen it, I urge you to watch it. I could write an entire chapter about the impact *Fight Club* had on my generation, but I'll leave that to the pop culture historians. Let's just say, in that time, after a few drinks, it'd be a perfectly reasonable request to ask someone to punch you in the face.

A line of angsty young women queued up to take a swing at this paragon of reckless manhood, and the punches began to land. Quinn and I each took a swing, but in our tipsy state, we barely clipped him. This tiny girl who'd been beaten by every man in her life unleashed a torrent against Blake's body, and he just took it, absorbing every punch like a statue. It was brutal and breathtaking to behold.

After a while, the punches stopped and the guests went back to dancing and drinking. Blake and I were left alone in the living room. I was deep in my cups and thinking about what I'd just witnessed. I told him, "I want you to punch me in the face."

He laughed.

I was 5'3" and 120 pounds. He was 6'4" and 195 pounds of pure construction man muscle. His fist was half the size of my skull. Obviously, it was the best idea I'd ever had.

"I've never been punched in the face," I pled. "If I'm going to be working with abused women, I should know what it feels like."

He kept saying no, but at some point I convinced him. We faced each other. I told him not to hold back, not to be a pussy.

I didn't even feel the punch.

The loud crack his knuckles made against my orbital bone brought everyone back into the room. By then, I was flat on my back, blood flowing down my face.

Blake picked me up, took me into the bathroom, and began cleaning the cut on my eyebrow. I was high from the adrenaline when he took my damaged face in his huge hands. He looked me dead straight in the eyes, and said, "Damn it, I think I love you."

I still have the scar.

Chapter Two

Ring of Fire

*S*hortly after Blake knocked me off my feet—quite literally—I ended it with Aden.

It wasn't because of any misconception that Blake was *the one*. He was supposed to be a good time, a rebound, a passionate fling, but definitely something temporary. Sure, I'd met his dad and his favorite aunt, and he built me a furniture fort, but he had plans to go on a world trip with two friends after spring semester, so he wasn't going to be around long anyway.

In the meantime, we watched obscure French movies and may have even done some hallucinogens together. You know, typical college dating stuff. We had this thing between us, whatever it was, but at that point, we hadn't even kissed.

Nothing serious happened until the day I left for winter break. We were hanging in my bedroom and decided to turn the awkward romantic tension into a game. We'd try to get as close as possible to each other without actually touching. The goal was to get the other person to lose their self-control. Alright, fine. The goal was to end up kissing, but without being the one to make the first move. Again, typical college dating stuff.

We knelt in front of each other on my bed, about half-a-foot between us to start. Slowly, we slid toward each other until the distance shrunk to a few inches. We swayed back and forth, advancing and retreating, until the gap between his lips and mine was as slim as an indiscretion. I still can't remember who "lost" the game, because when our lips finally connected, my mind was blown. It was the best kiss I'd had up until then.

I went home for a few weeks. We wrote each other letters and talked on the phone almost every day about all those things newly-infatuated fools talk about. Ourselves, each other, the world as we knew it. We said nothing and shared everything. On New Year's Day, after eight long hours in the car, I got back to my apartment and ran straight to my bedroom. Blake was waiting for me with his arms open, ready to catch me. We spent the rest of that January wearing each other out.

By then, I was experienced enough to know hormonal birth control and I would never be friends. We used condoms occasionally, but not all that often. Blake, having been raised in a traditional Catholic family, was taught to practice "natural family planning." The ol' rhythm method, the gist being to avoid having sex on fertile days. To do so, you need to count the days between cycles to figure out when it's safe. It's a lot of math. We both agreed that method wasn't very effective, and that the only real way to prevent an unplanned pregnancy was for his sperm not to enter my body. Pretty basic stuff, or so I thought.

Despite all of my presumed worldly wisdom, I was naïve enough to trust in my partner's self-hyped onanistic abilities to hold up his end of the bargain. Alas, there came a day when he decided *not* to interrupt our coitus, and when it happened, I swear I felt an electric shock go through my body. Like the universe had been altered and my life plans derailed. I asked him if he had any idea what he'd just done.

"Don't worry, I counted the days," he responded. "We should be fine."

"If you were counting on getting me pregnant, you couldn't have picked a better day!" I said.

Quinn bought me a pregnancy test a couple weeks later, then sat with me as we watched the little plus sign darken into an undeniable reality. If Quinn said anything, the words were lost in the fog of shock that engulfed me in that moment.

If you would've asked me at any point in my life before January 26, 2000 what to do if you found yourself pregnant with a guy you'd only known for a couple of months in the middle of college, I wouldn't have hesitated to say "get an abortion." I've always been pro-choice, and I have nothing but compassion for women who make that choice. When faced with my first positive pregnancy test, that option never even occurred to me.

My first thought was: *I need to meet with my advisor to figure out my class schedule, because I'm going to have a baby.* My second thought was: *I need to find an obstetrician because I need to make sure this baby is healthy.* Every decision I made from that point on centered on my child. I honestly did not know myself until that moment.

When I told Blake he'd be a dad, he sat down quickly, started smiling, and said, "Wow! This is really happening!" Then our relationship quickly began to shift.

Until that point, I'd been the focus of Blake's interest. But after I was pregnant, Blake was relieved. It was like he'd completed a task, and now he could focus on other things.

He once told me that before I got pregnant, he was afraid to fart around me. Once he knew I wasn't going anywhere, he could let it rip. Needless to say, any pretense of trying to win my affections were gone.

Our first real fight was two weeks later, on Valentine's Day, and its result set the tone moving forward. I'd bought him gifts, and wanted to be wined, dined, and adored. Blake responded by telling me that wasn't going to be part of his repertoire. I could forget about gifts, cards, flowers, or any kind of romance, especially on the "fake holidays" that were dictated by society. He told me the pressure to perform these acts of devotion on prescribed days made them feel false, that he wanted to express his care for me on a day-to-day basis.

And I went along with it. I convinced myself he was right, that those things *were* frivolous compared to his devotion in supporting me and this new life we'd created. Who needs flowers when they can give their baby a dad?

It wasn't like he was lazy. Blake told me that for him to be able to do his fatherly duty, he couldn't spend as much time with me as he had been. He'd need to focus on his studies and get back on the right track. He focused his energy on picking a major and going to classes, and it worked. He went from almost failing to making the Dean's list that semester.

Meanwhile, I was incubating a new human being.

Getting pregnant was ridiculously easy, but being pregnant was incredibly hard. I started throwing up almost immediately and didn't stop for the next four months. I had some spotting of blood around week eight that sent me to the doctor in a panic, and despite how miserable my body was feeling, my heart was relieved when the doctor told me the pregnancy was normal and I had no need for concerns. I kept promising the baby inside me that if they stuck with me, I'd stick with them.

Telling people about the pregnancy was more complicated than I'd anticipated. The people I thought would be difficult about it were actually the easiest to deal with. I quickly found out which friends wanted me around for me, and which just wanted Party Jess.

My first impression from Blake's family was that they were happy for us and would be helpful, but the reality was they simply weren't that involved in his life. Their enthusiastic response was really the indifference of spectators.

My family? Well, the Stout clan is made up of passionate, intense, and garrulous humans, and all that came out.

My parents, Rhett and Louise, were irate and humiliated at first. They took my unwed pregnancy very personally like most people of their generation would, like I'd done it just to shame them. I was on the receiving end of a lot of angry phone calls, incredibly thankful for the 500 miles between us.

Eventually, the anger subsided and was replaced with equally intense love. My parents became the most supportive and involved grandparents any child could ask for. I was their baby, and they loved me. They just did it sometimes in a volatile way.

Once it was obvious I wasn't going to lose the baby, my parents demanded that Blake and I get married. Rhett and Louise were relatively liberal, but old school when it came to the matters of bastards and public opinion.

"We don't care if you get divorced, but you need to be married when that baby is born," were their exact words. Then, they said they'd pay for the wedding. We had a decision to make.

Blake and I were still essentially strangers at that point. We started an inside joke that'd continue throughout our marriage. During moments of mundane intimacy—you know, those moments you see, like when two people who've bonded and have a family together automatically know exactly what the other partner needs—we'd just look at each other and say, "You don't know me." It was a way to cut straight through to the truth of the situation.

Here we were, together, navigating a world that was made of fog and mirrors. We knew I was having the baby. We knew we were in a relationship. We weren't living together, and a lot of the romance had died when I began throwing up daily.

We told my parents we had to think about it.

Blake and I talked the pros and cons of making our budding family legitimate, but in the end, we decided to leave it up to a game of cards.

Growing up, the women in my family played a game called Spite & Malice. It's essentially double solitaire, but the goal is more to screw the other person than it is to win the game. I taught it to Blake, and we decided that if I bested him three out of three times, we'd take my parents up on their free wedding offer. So, of course, that's how it went. Three for three. And for the rest of our marriage, we'd tell people it was one supported on the twin columns of spite and malice.

My mother planned her wedding in just under 10 weeks. Yes, "her" wedding. I'll take credit for the marriage, but the ceremony and reception was all hers. With the first problem she had to deal with being the top of my head.

I was a punk with a well-documented history of mohawks and chemically-altered hair. When you do that to your hair, you inevitably have to shave it all off and start fresh. The most recent time was in January, when Blake had shaved it all off in my bathroom, so I was completely shorn when my mother told me I had until Memorial Day to grow some *fucking* hair.

"Bald is beautiful," she said, "but it's not befitting for a bride."

While I urged my hair back into existence, my mother worked out the ceremonial details. She talked her pastor into marrying us in her church, despite neither of us practicing any faith. She booked a venue for the reception. She found all the vendors needed to pull off a respectable shotgun wedding: the photographer, the florist, the caterer. The woman was a whirlwind, which was great, because I'd never been the type of girl whose dream of a wedding day included doing endless hours of work. She did an amazing job, considering all the obstacles she had to negotiate.

The biggest one was my brother, Jack. Everyone in my family has strong personalities, but his has been the hardest to live with. The man covers his pain with thorns. Jack is caring, sensitive, and fragile. He's also intense, emotional, and unforgiving. Jack has a wicked temper, and often he couldn't contain or control it. As such, my parents and sister, Olivia, were terrified about how he'd respond to his baby sister getting pregnant unexpectedly.

We hid the truth from him for as long as possible, but this kind of secret could only be kept for so long. Babies are an undeniable truth that get bigger every day. When we finally told him, his brittle crust cracked and a hot rage came pouring through. He was mad I was irresponsible enough to get pregnant in the first place. He was frustrated he didn't have more control over me, or at least the choices I made. And he really did not like the sudden influx of so many strangers into his family. He thought I was ruining my life and hurting our family in the process.

Eventually, the anger burned away and he accepted this new reality. He agreed to be a groomsman.

The next issue to tackle was my expanding waistline. There was no denying I had a bun in the oven, and I needed to find a wedding dress that minimized my belly. It's challenging, to say the least. No empire waists or fitted dresses would do the job! Mom, Olivia, and I eventually found a giant bell-shaped dress that managed to cover every sign of sin. At first glance, at least.

Most of the wedding was like this—covering up facts and presenting a good show. Deep down underneath the pomp and subterfuge, there were moments of sincerity and sacred truths.

The wedding was a quick and simple affair. I was covered in lace and fake nails, standing in a church I had no belief in across from a man I barely knew. However, I knew the commitment to making a family was real. The reception was a luncheon at the yacht club. We had a horrible DJ, but that didn't stop me from dancing with everyone. My brother danced with me that day and told me he loved me. It's a moment I'll always cherish, especially now, during these years of silence between us. (I'll explain that issue later.) Blake even danced, despite loathing it. Looking back on our marriage now, it was the only time he danced with me.

My favorite photo from the night is of me sitting at the head table, holding Blake's hand to my stomach as our baby girl did flips inside of me.

After the wedding, Blake dropped me off in Mankato and headed to Coon Rapids. He lived with his dad and worked construction, while I spent the summer taking classes and living with another man, my roommate.

"Just Jack." We called him that because we both had brothers named Jack, so he wasn't my Jack or Blake's Jack. He was Just Jack.

I needed a place for the summer. At the end of the spring semester, the lease for the apartment I had been renting with a group of girls was up and we all scattered for various reasons. The plan was my budding family was gonna move in with my parents for the fall semester; my college advisor helped me rearrange my class schedule to accommodate taking off the fall semester, so I'd graduate only one semester behind—and

Blake's older brother was ditching Just Jack with three months left on the lease. It worked perfectly. His only stipulation was that he didn't want to have to get me pickles and ice cream in the middle of the night. I agreed.

Just Jack was single at the time, and occasionally brought his dates home. Every time he did, I'd waddle out of my room on cue with my enormous baby belly, and shout, "Oh Jack, you promised you wouldn't bring 'em home anymore!"

He kept the woman that laughed, and now they have three beautiful girls of their own. He was one of the best roommates I've ever had.

Blake and I saw each other on the weekends he wasn't working. The summer passed quickly. On the last week of August, I moved back into my high school bedroom in Springfield, Illinois. Blake joined me in mid-September. He found a construction job to last him through the holidays, and I tried not to think about how this creature inside me would exit.

I was happy to be back home. My oldest best friend, Iris, still lived there, so we spent time together figuring out what it means to be a momma. Iris had been at the parenting game for a couple of years already. She had her oldest, Elise, when she was nineteen. I'd held Iris's hand as that baby girl came into the world. She'd just had her second child, Robert, a few weeks earlier. Watching Iris be a mom helped keep my fears at bay. She told me that I'd be great, and I believed her.

I had an epiphany early on in my pregnancy while I was taking a bath. I was watching my stomach writhe from my baby's alien movements, and it dawned on me then, on a molecular level, my life was no longer my own. That it'd never been mine. That every decision I made, every action I took, affected this person I was growing. Until that moment, I hadn't realized how connected we all are. I saw the web of humanity stretching from me to my mother to my grandmother, and back to my child. It was enlightening and grounding at the same time.

Then, on to the next battle. Naming a person is intimidating as hell. We had a boy's name picked out almost immediately, because I was convinced I'd have nothing but boys. I simply wasn't equipped to raise girls.

I'd never worn makeup, and I can't braid hair. I'm a tomboy. What would I do with a girl? When my new doctor in Springfield wanted her own ultrasound pictures, we found out the gender of our baby. She was a she! We had three weeks to name her.

Blake was not helpful. He shot down every name I thought of, never offering his own suggestions. We were two weeks into this battle when we went to the grocery store and I spied a booklet entitled, *Name Your Child According to Their Zodiac Sign!* I grabbed it, shoved it at him, and told him to look for ideas.

He asked me what her sign would be, and I told him she'd be a Libra. Amara was the first name in that section, so he said, "Let's name her Amara."

I wanted to disagree—this was the first input he'd given at all, so I wanted to shoot it down just to keep things somewhat even—but then he told me that Amara means "eternal beauty."

"If she looks anything like her mother, she will be beautiful," he said.

Well, that did it. I was a sucker for his charms. Now that we had a name for our offspring, all there was left to do was wait for her escape from my womb.

Mothers love to trade war stories about deliveries, so here are some of mine: I'd gone in the week before with false labor and was sent home. The rejection made me question every bit of confidence I had in knowing my body. On October 4th, I started having contractions, but tried to ignore them. I wasn't falling for that trick again.

After dinner that night, I threw up, and for the next 24 hours I'd have the joy of vomiting every time I dilated. After something horrible and alien fell out of my vagina—later, I was told that thing was the mucus plug—I decided it was time to take this horror show to a hospital.

We got to the birth center around ten at night, and they decided I wasn't dilated high enough to earn a room. I got parked in triage for hours, where I screamed and cried because of the horrendous back labor Amara was putting me through. When they finally gave me a room and an epidural, I passed out.

Without me at the wheel, labor continued to progress, as these things do. At some point, they broke my water and saw meconium in it. That meant she pooped and was basically breathing in her own shit.

Blake was with me through the entire experience, but he was more interested in the biology involved than in the spirituality of his daughter's birth. At some point, he and a nurse lifted me up and literally folded me in half in an attempt to get our stubborn girl out. I was so thankful for the nurse who stayed with me past her shift. I think she knew I needed someone to be there with me, emotionally and physically.

Finally, I dilated enough to start pushing. I pushed for three hours. And Amara, evidently thinking she hadn't made things dramatic enough, threw in a couple of possibly fatal risks at the finish line.

By the time it was all over, Amara had survived having the cord wrapped around her neck, along with not one, but two knots in her cord. The doctor later told me that any one of those things could have killed her during the delivery. In the end, the stubborn girl made it into the world.

Amara Rose Schaffhausen was born on October 5, 2000 at 3:40 p.m. She looked like a mole with a huge shock of dark hair, and her face was all smooshed from being stuck in the birth canal for so long. She was the most beautiful thing I'd ever seen.

They whisked her away as soon as she was born, and my heart stopped until she was back in my arms.

Blake was fascinated by the whole process, even disappointed he didn't get to cut the umbilical cord or see the placenta. He was amazed by Amara, at how tiny yet strong she was. Blake was comfortable holding her and not the least bit squeamish. After she was born, he stayed around for a couple of hours, then left the hospital to run errands.

When the doctors finally brought Amara back after making sure she was okay, I held her for hours. I never wanted to put her down. I slept with my body curved around hers, breathing in her exhalations, trying to keep that lost feeling of being whole. I wanted so badly to put her back inside me, back where I could keep her safe.

Chapter Three

Brown Eyed Girl

There are a thousand and one clichés about becoming a mother, and I'm here to tell you that every single one of them is true.

When Amara came into my life, I was truly in love for the first time. I couldn't get enough of my little pixie girl. I would stare at her for hours and gush over every little detail, from her coos to her poos. When her soulful brown eyes fastened onto mine, I knew my only purpose in life was to love her. Amara Rose captivated my heart and beguiled my every sense with her mere presence in this world.

One of those days in full-gush mode, I turned to Blake and said, "Don't you just love her? Isn't she amazing?"

"If I was even half as into her as you are, I wouldn't be able to work," he responded. "I just don't feel the same way."

That didn't mean he didn't love her. Because he did. He loved us all as much as he was capable of loving anyone. He found her to be interesting, and he wore the mantle of dad comfortably—as long as it didn't require too much out of him.

After Amara's birth, and with the wedding behind us, my parents stepped up in a big way. Primarily, they let us live with them for free for almost four months and save up money. It was a blessing to have my parents letting us join them for dinners and an extra set of arms to snuggle

Amara while I showered. They gave me the support and time I needed to master breastfeeding, co-sleeping, and baby-wrangling 101 before I had to figure out how to do all that *plus* homemaking and Social Work 301 after the three of us were released back into the wilds of Minnesota.

On New Year's Day, 2001 we settled into a new apartment in Mankato before starting a new college semester. We couldn't afford childcare, so Blake and I picked our class schedules to guarantee that one of us would always be home with Amara.

The plan worked early on, but after the first month, it fell apart. Blake told me he needed more time in the library to study, and before I knew it, I was taking Amara to nearly every one of my classes.

One night, I took her to my School Social Work class. I'd always been an involved student, and especially enjoyed debating during lectures, so of course, at some point, I was passionately arguing with my professor while breastfeeding Amara. I don't remember the specific topic we were discussing, but do remember my professor's face just as I was about to make a vital point. Her expression was a look of abject weariness but quickly morphed into complete shock. Amara had unlatched from my breast and stretched herself out, completely exposing me to the classroom.

I stopped my argument mid-word, frantically turned around as I tried to pull my shit together, and whispered to Quinn, "I think I just flashed the teacher."

"Well, now you're flashing me," she said. "Put that thing away before someone gets hurt."

Overall, my teachers and classmates were supportive of the tiny inquisitive intruder I brought along. Amara loved being in the classroom. She enjoyed learning, and was precocious in every aspect, including moving around. She was rolling over by two weeks, and crawling before most babies even considered how to get from point A to point B. Fortunately, I got through the semester before she learned how to walk. Barely…

Meanwhile, Blake was having a hard time getting back into the swing of classes. It was difficult for him to focus on his work with Amara and I around, so, he told me that's why he needed to spend time at his friend's place or at the library. I figured to each their own devices and didn't worry. I wasn't his mother. Just his wife.

Sometime after midterms, he let it slip that his friend had dropped out of school and wasn't even going to work anymore. This couldn't be the end of the story, so I started asking digging questions. Was he into drugs? Was he depressed? Blake said, "No, no, nothing that serious." His friend was just consumed with playing an online roleplaying game called *Everquest* and had stopped leaving the house. This was the first time I'd ever heard of the game. I asked Blake to explain it.

As he was telling me how this was one of the first-of-its kind games where you play online with other people, it dawned on me that perhaps all those hours Blake said he was studying in a baby-free zone were really being poured into virtual-questing for swords and spells.

I confronted him directly. "Have you been playing this game, too?"

He said yes, and then told me that gaming with his friends was having a negative effect on his schooling. He was barely passing his classes again, and he admitted he hadn't been writing his English papers for some time.

While Blake had always been incredibly brilliant at math and science, he'd completely shut down when he had to write a paper. To help him, I offered to edit his papers.

One day, I watched him try to work on his paper. He obsessively wrote and re-wrote the same introductory paragraph over and over again, like a vinyl record player's needle stuck in a groove. It took hours for him just to get a few words down. Watching him struggle, I knew editing wasn't going to be enough. So, I did the only thing I could think of— write his papers for him.

That was only one of the painful adjustments that came with living together for the first time. I was also becoming increasingly frustrated with what I saw as a lack of participation on his part in household duties.

One day, I walked into the kitchen to find Blake holding Amara in his arms. He told me that he'd cleaned the kitchen. To him, this meant wiping counters off with a dishcloth.

In response, I detailed the 16 steps I took to *actually* clean the kitchen. When I started talking to him about the need to use actual cleaning products, he said he didn't want to use poisonous chemicals in his kitchen. It was then that I noticed the pack of cigarettes nestled in his front jacket pocket, and I snapped.

I went to grab the cigarettes, to yell at him for the hypocrisy of filling his body with chemicals, but as I reached for them, my thumbnail scratched Amara's face.

There was a horrible pregnant pause as Amara registered this new sensation of pain and then broke the silence with a wail of disbelief.

Instantly, I fell apart. I crumbled to the floor, sobbing about how my baby girl had gotten scratched because I couldn't manage my home. I told Blake we needed to see a counselor to help us figure out how to make this marriage work. He agreed to give it a shot.

Throughout the sessions, I described to the counselor my expectations for maintaining our home. Raised by neat freaks, I believed the house should be scrubbed top to bottom every other week. More importantly, I wanted Amara to have a clean, safe, and peaceful place to grow and develop. I also grew up on mandatory family dinners at the dining table and wanted us all, at the very least, to have those same dinners together. In counseling, I was looking for a third party to tell me if I was being unrealistic or to tell Blake to step up and participate more. But that's not how counseling works...

The therapist worked with me to grasp the idea that treating someone the way you wanted to be treated didn't automatically make them treat you the same way. She also encouraged us to focus on how our strengths lined up with each other's weaknesses, instead of trying to make the other person our replica. By the end of the third session, our roles were much more clear: Blake would provide for the house and I'd have complete dominion over how it was managed.

But whenever I clearly communicated my needs, Blake responded with his own unwillingness to meet those needs. What I saw was the best he could offer, he said, and I could choose to accept it or leave him. There was no room for negotiation.

Why did I accept him for who he was? Why didn't I pack up the baby and hit the road? There are no simple answers, but I'll try to explain my thought process at the time.

I was twenty-two years old, ridiculously close to graduating from college. I was driven by a desire to be with my daughter all the time and do whatever it took to give her the best chance. I was so afraid to admit to myself that I was in a less-than-stellar marriage, and there was a part of me that believed I was getting what I deserved. Does that sound harsh? Maybe a little familiar? Through the gifts of age, therapy, and devastating loss I have learned that some things are worth fighting for. And sometimes, that means fighting the demons in my own psyche whispering that I should settle for the safety of status quo instead of striving for the possibility of growing towards the light. I had to learn that I had to value myself the way I wanted my daughter to value herself someday. But in 2001, I was still locked in a mental cage built by society perhaps, but I was the one with the keys. I just didn't know it yet. So, I decided I needed to lower my expectations, just do the best with the cards I'd been dealt. My motto for the next decade would be: *This is the bed I made; I'm going to have to sleep in it!*

After he *barely* passed his spring semester classes, Blake did some calculations about our family budget and his immediate earning potential in the construction field. We decided together our little family would be better off if he put college on hold and went back to construction work. I was on track to graduate with honors in December, but there was no job I could do in the meantime that would cover daycare costs, plus a little extra. I was looking at three whole months of loving up on Amara Rose all day, every day until the fall, when I'd start an internship with the Hennepin Public Defenders office in Minneapolis, where Blake could pick up work with his old construction company. Big city living in the Twin Cities was our family's next step.

We moved to Minneapolis in May of 2001. We found a cozy apartment built into the back of a Victorian home in a quaint residential neighborhood. I savored every moment with Amara Rose. She started walking when she was eight months old and began to dance shortly thereafter. Every day with her was an adventure often harrowing, frequently comedic, and usually pretty sticky. She wasn't very snuggly as that required staying still. But she was sweet and affectionate. Amara was adept at the flyby kisses and body slam hugs as she moved around the room finding furniture to climb or a toy to dismantle.

Blake worked long hours doing as many side jobs as he could. When he was home, he indulged in his computer game habit, leaving Amara and I to spend time by ourselves. While that was bliss, many of the patterns that would persist throughout our marriage were established during these early months.

Blake worked, and I managed the money and did all the household duties. Most of the time, Amara and I spent our days without him. He'd show for special occasions and gave us just enough affection and attention to keep us all connected. Blake liked having us in the background to give him an identity, without us demanding much in return. He'd take us off the shelf to play with once in a while, but for the most part, we were free to carry on without him.

Whenever I contemplated his contributions to our family, I mentally credited him with every hour he spent working was an hour he spent *for* his family. It helped me cope with the loneliness I often battled. And it worked. For a while.

When Amara was ten months old, I went to work full-time at my senior internship, which meant I had to leave her in someone else's care. Blake's Aunt Betty offered to be our daycare provider. She lived in a multigenerational house that was a remnant from a bygone era. Amara's great-grandma lived in a back room, while the rest of the house overflowed with Betty's six children and one grandson, Ryan, who was a couple months older than Amara.

Everyone adored Amara, and she never lacked for attention or stimulation, so it became very hard for me to leave my baby with anyone else, especially after four years of classes devoted to all the horrible things that happen to people. I could trust Betty to care for Amara like she was her own grandchild, and she was willing to watch her for a fraction of what we'd have to pay otherwise. Amara was truly blessed to spend her first years being cared for by Betty and her tumultuous crew.

Looking back on those months, I have no idea how I managed to take care of Amara and get through school at the same time, but somehow, I figured it out. Being a mother gave me a focus and purpose I hadn't had before. For example, while many of my peers spent their spring break on a Cancun beach, I spent it writing my senior thesis. My time was suddenly very valuable and in high demand, and in response, I developed exceptional organizational skills that have benefited me more as a professional than any other job experience.

I graduated from MNSU Cum Laude that December 2001, and in January, I began my first professional job. I worked as a case manager for a guardianship and conservatorship company. It's a niche social work job most people aren't aware of exists. Some people, for reasons of disease or disability, can't make their own decisions. When they're found to be "incompetent" by a court, they have to be placed under conservatorship or guardianship. The company I worked for was the technical guardian, but as case manager, I fulfilled the legal requirements to make decisions for those special needs individuals. Whenever I tried to describe my job to someone, Blake let me ramble on until they glazed over, and then he'd cut in and say, "She puts little old ladies in nursing homes."

Life carried on as it had, except now I was working fulltime while still doing *everything* for Amara, and around the house. Blake was steadily working his way up to foreman, and still took every side construction job he could find. When he had free time at home, he was mastering another game on his computer.

We spent a year in that cozy Minneapolis apartment, but as our lease was coming due for renewal, we started thinking about owning rather than renting. I was bringing in an income now, and Blake had been getting one raise after another. He'd been spending his days building other people's houses, so he understood the value as an investment as well as a necessity.

We picked a random realtor and went on a whirlwind tour of more houses than I care to remember. In about two weeks, we found our first home—a modest split-entry in Farmington, Minnesota. We closed on it just in time to celebrate our second wedding anniversary.

The house had a lot of potential for sweat equity, and Blake was both motivated and capable of doing the work. I was happy to be moving to a suburb where Amara could run around in a huge yard with neighborhood friends. It was also big enough to accommodate more people, which was important, because *I wanted to make more people*. Amara was almost two years old, and I was jonesing for another baby. Blake wanted at least three years between kids, so I did my best to ride out the hormonal wave I was on.

Luckily, Amara kept my baby fever at bay by being a fantastic distraction. I know I'm biased, but she was a blast to hang out with. Watching her acquire new skills every day was riveting. Her complex personality was there from her first breath and grew as she did. She was inquisitive and fearless. She just had to see what was around the next corner, under the filthiest rock, or in the back of the darkest closet she could find. Amara loved all people, young or old, beautiful or maimed, whole or broken. It didn't matter to her. We were all fascinating creatures here for her to figure out.

Amara was wicked smart from birth. She began using full sentences when she was eighteen months old. Most toddlers make demands with as few words as possible, but not Amara. She used as many words as she possibly could. Instead of "food mama," she'd say, "I'm hungry. What do we have to eat?" She would talk to anyone who'd listen. In fact, she'd keep talking long after whoever it was she was having a conversation with had left the room.

She was also ridiculously petite. Amara fell off the growth charts by the time she was four months old and wouldn't make it back until she was in elementary school. It was an odd juxtaposition. She looked like a fairy and spoke like an adult.

One day, when she was around two years old, I took her to the neighborhood playground. She was strong and athletic, and scaled the advanced climbing structures like a billy goat. Because Amara looked like a small one-year-old, the other mothers there were having heart palpitations waiting for her to fall. When she was finally finished, she jumped down with ease, ran over to me, and said in her squeaky sweet voice, "Mommy, I'm parched. Do you have any water to drink?" Of course, I had some on hand to give her. Conquering the world is thirsty work.

She was adorably frustrating to discipline. I'd put her in a timeout for some indiscretion, most often for doing something she was explicitly told not to do, like climbing a bookcase or talking back. When I told her she was free to go, her response was, "That's okay, I am fine here."

Then, she'd stay at least as long as her timeout was supposed to last, as if she was pointing out how ineffective the punishment was.

Amara was a logical child, prone to many in-depth discussions. Most children will try to prolong bedtime by requesting more drinks of water or food, but not her. At three, she'd figured out that if she asked me a question about religion or sociology, she'd be able to stay up at least a half-hour longer.

"Mommy, why doesn't everyone get to live in a house like us?" she'd ask. "Mom, do you think wolves have souls? Momma, what happens when we die?"

I had the tools to answer questions like "Why is the sky blue?" but these questions rooted in faith versus facts I am still exploring myself. I met this curious creature where she was at in her journey and shared my thoughts as best I could. "No one really knows what happens when we die," I'd explained to her. "It's the last big adventure."

At a development age when most moms are worried about their kids crawling out of their crib, I was terrified of Amara sneaking out of the house. She was a monkey who climbed with little fear. When she was nine months old, she'd figured out how to push chairs around and use them to climb onto the top of the stove and kitchen counters. We were forced to adapt. We didn't have kitchen chairs from the time she was nine months old until she was eighteen months.

More worrisome were those times when, as a toddler, she'd creep out of her room at night, go into the kitchen, and take knives out of the drawers. I never heard a peep. Later, I'd find them under her bed.

When I asked her why she was smuggling cutlery into her room, she looked me dead in the eye like I was a bit slow and said, "You won't let me play with them in the kitchen." She was right about that.

As I was trying to keep knives away from Amara, Blake excelled at his job. The housing boom was in full swing, and he reaped in on the benefits. He helped construct custom homes, and quickly became a foreman and trainer for the company he worked for. The promotions and bonuses gave him the gratification he needed, while the custom homes were challenging enough to keep him stimulated. He even won a state championship for a construction competition. In March of 2003, his company sent us to San Diego to compete in the Nationals, where he had to take written exams and participate in competitive building events. This trip was the closest thing to a honeymoon we ever got.

My sister took Amara for the week, so for once, it was the two of us. However, Blake was too worried about the competition to enjoy the trip, so my plan to get another baby out of the deal was a bust. Blake placed in the top 10%, but alas, didn't win. He was incredibly disappointed. He never talked to me about how he felt, but I noticed a bitterness begin to grow where his pride had been. He blamed his loss on a perceived bias within the national competition itself. The company he worked for was a small local business, and all the winners were from large national companies that also happened to fund the event. I don't know. Maybe he had a point.

Once we were home and back in the old rhythm of work and life again, I approached him about making Amara a big sister. The results were not pleasant.

Sex is so much more complicated than Hollywood leads you to believe. Growing up, I was told that guys always wanted it, and gals had to beat them off with a stick. In reality, we're all just people ruled by hormones, emotions, and needs that we rarely have any insight about. Throughout our marriage, sex was more of a battleground than a place for us to connect. I consistently had a higher sex drive than he did, and I learned very early on that if he had the choice between spending time with me or a video game, the game was going to win every time. I knew if he wasn't interested I shouldn't set myself up for rejection, but I had this very insistent and loud biological clock ticking in my ear that drowned out any emotional self-preservation I had.

One day, I let him know as diplomatically as possible that I was done waiting, and it was time for him to ante up. He did so, grudgingly, and immediately after started a fight.

In hindsight, my method of demanding he put out and making him feel guilty for not having a higher sex drive was like poking a pissed-off rattlesnake with a stick. Blake was a man whose pride had already been hit, and here I was, pressuring him into sex. In bed afterwards, both of us lying there naked, he lashed out at me.

I hadn't yet gotten my pre-baby physique back after Amara, though I had been working on it. He grabbed my belly and told me I was too fat to have another baby. He said he wouldn't have sex with me again until I'd lost 20 pounds.

Talk about an emotional gut punch. I was humiliated and felt powerless. I swore he'd never see me naked again, but that wasn't very practical. We didn't speak to each other for two weeks.

We'd barely started talking again when Amara and I left to go on an epic journey to see extended family for the Easter holiday. One of the first stops was a visit to Ida, Michigan, "the center of the world," according to my father, a place where we share genetics with more of the population than we don't.

I showed Amara off to all of my dad's relatives. We went to the nursing home to visit my great-uncle Heinrich, an amputee who delighted in frightening small children by removing his prosthetic leg and waving his stump at them. When he did it for my two-and-a-half-year-old, rather than horror, Amara squealed with delight and began rubbing his stump in amazement. Uncle Heinrich was disappointed. When she asked if she could play with his fake leg, he frowned and told her no. Poor Heinrich.

After our adventures in Ida, Grandpa Rhett and Amara dropped me in Chicago so I could visit my brother Jack. After a day of catching up sans my miniature motormouth, Jack and I headed down to rendezvous with the rest of the family for Easter. I was double-checking my itinerary on the ride when it dawned on me that I probably should've had a period during the trip. I counted the days, and they weren't adding up. I woke up Easter morning and took a pregnancy test, not thinking it'd be positive. We'd only had sex that one time, and it wasn't during a particularly promising time frame. Another plus sign came back, and there she was—Sophie.

I called Blake and told him the news. It was hard to tell what he was feeling from his response. Mostly, it seemed like he was surprised it happened so easily again. He was happy, and not angry I didn't wait until we were in the same state again before I took the test. He quickly did some math and told me that our Easter present would show up around Christmas.

Pregnancy number two tried to kill me right from conception. I started puking almost immediately and didn't stop for nine months. I threw up so violently that I broke blood vessels in my face and my eyes several times a month. I was working as an Adult Mental Health Case Manager at the time, and any chance of waiting to tell my coworkers and clients that I was pregnant went out the window as soon as I showed up to work looking like my eyes were bleeding. My skin had a noticeable green hue, and my eyes literally had no white left to show. They were completely blood red. One schizophrenic client thought his meds had stopped working and he was hallucinating. Poor man.

One day, I was laying on the couch, dying from this new life growing inside of me, when Blake walked in.

"I don't think I can do this!" I said. "I can't take care of everything and be this sick."

He looked at me, took a deep breath, and spoke in his calm and matter-of-fact tone. "You wanted to have another baby, Jess. You knew it would make you sick. You have to just suck it up."

I felt stupid for even asking for his sympathy.

The next day, the midwives put me on daily IV treatments. I would come home from work, hook myself up to a bag of fluids, and stay connected until I left the next morning. It took six weeks until I was able to stay hydrated and keep food down. I sucked it up, and did what needed to be done, but knew deep in my core that I was on my own.

Around this time, Aunt Betty let me know she wasn't going to be able to watch Amara *and* a new baby, so I started looking for a daycare. I was shocked by how expensive it was. I made $14.00 an hour as a licensed social worker and there was a years-long wage freeze at the non-profit I worked for, so I quickly figured I didn't make enough money to justify working. When I laid the numbers out for Blake, he agreed we'd be better off if I stayed home. The decision was made: I wouldn't return to work after the birth, and would eventually watch other children to supplement our income.

As I settled into the process of preparing to leave the workforce, it was time to get this baby out of me.

My kitchen has always been my refuge. Even when I'm not an emotional mess, I'm very particular about who can invade that space. Generally, it was easy enough to fend off intruders, but that Christmas, Blake's mom, Darcy, had come to stay with us. Shortly after she arrived, my blood pressure went up enough that the midwives put me on bedrest.

On Christmas Day, I was in the kitchen holding a couple of brand-new pans I'd gotten as presents, wanting desperately to hide them so Darcy wouldn't use, or potentially ruin, them. I was four days from my due date and may not have been in the most rational state of mind. My kitchen was a complete mess: a pan of burned eggs left on the burner, sink overflowing with dirty dishes, milk left to sour. I felt violated and out of control.

I hugged my new cookware to my chest and began to weep big fat tears of frustration and rage. Blake came in, gave me a hug, and said, "Don't worry, the baby will be here soon."

Two days later, I woke with contractions. They came and went with no regularity.

On December 27th, one of Blake's many cousins was getting married. I decided that although the contractions didn't seem to be progressing, I was in no mood to go to a wedding, so I stayed home with Amara. As soon as Blake and his mom left, the contractions got more persistent.

I tried to keep the pain from Amara, and not let my worry that Blake wouldn't come back in time infect our last few hours as a twosome. I read her stories and we built towers with blocks. She always preferred activity toys like puzzles or blocks versus imaginative toys like baby dolls. (But she did have her stuffed elephant, Eli, whom she was devoted to from birth to death.)

I put the book of Chinese fairytales I had just finished back on the shelf that hung above her bed. A twin with a headboard decorated with delicate pink roses just big enough to accommodate my painfully pregnant body. As I watched Amara add another tower to her city made of blocks, I tried to talk to her about what it'd be like to have a baby sister. We talked about how babies cry a lot and need to be taken care of, and eventually she made the connection to Eli, who also needed to be loved and cared for. Amara told me not to worry, that she'd help with the baby as soon as she got out of my belly. Then, she asked me how exactly the baby was going to get out.

"Mommy doesn't want to think about that right now, sweetness," I said. "Why don't you find another book for me."

Chapter Four

Float On

$\mathcal{S}$hortly after Blake and I walked through the hospital doors, we were admitted to a room. Shortly after, the midwife came in to see how far dilated I was. I wasn't too far along yet, she decided, and stood to leave.

At that exact moment, I heard a popping noise.

"Anyone else hear that?" I asked the room, to no replies.

Then I felt it. My water had broken. It spewed out of my body like a geyser and covered the midwife head to toe. She wiped the worst of the watery goop off with a towel, and nonchalantly announced that things should move steadily along now.

It was a fitting start to a messy and dramatic life.

Part of me worried that the complications I'd had with Amara had resulted from using so many medical interventions, and this time, I was determined for the birth to be "natural."

At the time, it was all the rage to soak in warm water to ease the pain of contractions. The hospital I was in was rather old, and the tub they had was a basic 1970s avocado bathtub—very low to the ground without a lot of room for floating. So, when the contractions came, rather than calling for an epidural, I got naked and dipped myself into the puddle.

Once I squeezed myself inside, I started getting what I like to call "real contractions." They're the "holy fuck, where's my fucking epidural?" contractions.

There I was: naked, writhing in pain, screaming and cussing up a goddamn storm. Blake tried to hoist me out of the tub, but by that point I was too slippery and enormously large to move, so we waited for the contraction to stop. When we finally got me back onto the bed, a nurse called for the epidural.

As I waited for what seemed like years for the anesthesiologist to get to the room, I gritted my teeth and tried to utilize those breathing techniques they taught in all those Lamaze classes I never got around to taking. When the anesthesiologist finally arrived, I almost wept. The contractions felt like someone was stabbing me with knives from the inside, but thankfully, they dulled with the injection. The pain of a needle being shoved into my spine was nothing compared to the pain of my body trying to expel another human being.

From the moment we entered the hospital to the time her little head was crowning, it took my new baby only four hours to get out, a sprint compared to Amara's marathon. I pushed for a blurry half hour, it was over, and there she was: my Sophie Marie, conceived in anger and determination, but loved all the same.

We'd known for months that we were having another girl, but yet again, we came up short in the name department. She was eighteen hours old when we decided on Sophie Marie, after the book *Sophie's World* by Jostein Gaarder, a novel about the history of philosophy, and still one of my favorites. I looked forward to reading it with her someday, maybe when she was in junior high, but never got the chance.

She came into this world round, bald, and blue-eyed. Blake was ecstatic that he got to cut the cord and poke at the placenta this time.

My new life as a stay-at-home mom was welcomed with a vicious cold spell that trapped us inside the Farmington house for the first weeks of 2004. I'd been living in the Frozen North long enough to know that the cold can always get colder, but a static temperature of negative 20 took things to a new level. At the same time, I was learning that a second child takes things to a whole new level of parenting.

My heart quickly adapted to the increase in love that Sophie brought, but my body failed to grow the extra set of arms I needed. When I was younger, I thought the coolest superpower would be the ability to speak to animals, but as a twenty-four-year-old mother of two, all I wanted was to replicate myself a hundred times over. One Jess to cook the food, one Jess to nurse the baby, one Jess to read stories to the preschooler, and a few more to deal with the biological functions of her own body.

Since I couldn't clone myself, luckily, my family came to the rescue yet again. During the first weeks of Sophie's life, my parents and brother came to clean my house, stock my shelves, and snuggle my offspring. I'll never forget the sight of Rhett vacuuming out my cupboards as the perpetual bachelor Jack soothed a wailing baby and Grandma Louise directed everyone from her kitchen table perch.

"Rhett, you missed the top shelf," she said, coffee in hand. "Jessica, why don't you take a shower? Amara, bring Grandma her knitting."

To help me through the chaos, my sister Olivia took Amara back to South Dakota for a three-week visit. I missed Amara, but knew she was getting an opportunity to forge bonds with her auntie and her cousin, Anne. For instance, only in South Dakota could Amara drink juice out of wine glasses, hot tub in the snow, and choke wild geese.

Let me explain that last one.

One day, when they were all out at a local park, Olivia took Amara and Anne to feed a gaggle of geese. Now, one would suspect a child of such diminutive size to be intimidated by a hissing goose, but not Amara. After feeding one, she felt the goose was ungrateful and rude, and thus, in need of a lesson. She walked right up to that goose, grabbed it by the neck, and yelled at it to be nice—or so, I was told much later. Fortunately, Olivia stepped in before any permanent damage was done.

Weeks later, when my sister brought my first love back to me on Valentine's Day, she told me to invest in toddler-sized riot gear to protect Amara from her own future recklessness.

While Amara was making a reputation for herself one state over, Sophie and I were getting to know each other. As newborns, Sophie was diametrically opposed to Amara in almost every way, one of the most obvious being her feeding rituals. I breastfed all of my children, but Sophie was the only one who refused to ever take a bottle. Not once. We tried every type of bottle and nipple available, including a bottle that looked exactly like a boob, but even that didn't work.

Among other things, this pickiness meant I could never leave her alone for very long. At best, she'd go hungry, and at worst, she'd try to get her own food—once with an extremely painful result.

When she was a year old, Blake and I left her with my mother for 36 hours. The whole family was in Springfield, Illinois for the Christmas holidays. So, Blake and I left the kiddos with Grandma and Grandpa and headed up to Chicago. We stayed at Jack's place and caught a Blue Man show and had a fancy dinner out. That lone night we were gone, Grandma Louise let Sophie sleep in her bed. Everything started out fine, but sometime around 3 a.m., Sophie crawled up her grandmother's nightgown and latched onto the body part where she'd been taught her food came from. No need to get into specifics, other than to say there was agony on one side and frustration on the other. Needless to say, they were both ecstatic to see me the next afternoon.

Later in life, Sophie delighted in making people squirm with this tale, always ending it with an unnecessary, but completely perfect, closing line.

"That's right," she'd say. "I tried to suck on my grandma's boob."

The picky eating was consistent throughout Sophie's life. Once, when she was four, I made her a ham and cheese sandwich for lunch, and cut it into the shape of a star. I left her at the table to eat, but from the other room I heard the distinctive sound of my kitchen garbage can opening and closing. I walked to the trash and saw she'd dumped her entire lunch.

I let her know right then and there that she wasn't getting anything else to eat until dinner. She didn't like that, and immediately asked for yogurt. I said no. She waited five minutes and asked again.

"Can I have yogurt?"

"No."

She waited another five minutes and asked again, with the same result. This lasted for three hours.

Finally, I caved.

She took one spoonful of the yogurt and looked at me with a smirk. "Nevermind," she said. "I don't want it anymore."

My eye began to twitch with pure frustration. As calmly as I could, I said, "Sophie, you'll eat that yogurt, or I will spank your butt so hard you won't be able to sit for a week!"

She looked at me, then at the yogurt, then back at me.

"Go ahead and spank me," she dared me calmly as can be. "I am not eating that yogurt."

I knew this was a pivotal moment in parenting and that if I didn't follow through with consequences, I would lose what little integrity I had. Obviously, she considered eating the yogurt the worst repercussion... I held her nose and force-fed her the entire carton. This happened a few times, but when it did, Sophie was so completely obstinate that, even when I'd physically overpower her, she'd somehow defy the reality of my dominance. I could never win with her. She would drive me to do things I swore I would never do, like threaten physical violence, while she always remained faithful to her character. In that respect, she was more like me than I ever imagined she would be.

Sleep was another battlefield. Sophie didn't sleep a full night through until she was two years old. This meant I'd wake up several times a night to negotiate with a miniature terrorist whose main tool of torture was sleep deprivation.

First, I'd try to get her settled into her own bed. When that didn't work, I'd try to get her to sleep with me in my bed. When that didn't work either, I'd put her back into her own bed. Finally, I'd give up and make coffee to start another sleep-deprived day.

Later in her life, after she finally hit that much-delayed milestone of sleeping through the night, I'd often wake to find her standing by my side of the bed, just staring at me. Sophie could be downright creepy. (Meanwhile, Blake never got up through any of it. He slept through it all.)

The kid was also straight up bold. At some point, Sophie learned how to make her eyes appear ten times bigger than they were and used this trick to mystify unwary adults into giving her things, mostly junk food. When she was a toddler, she'd walk up to unsuspecting adults, tug their shirts to get their full attention, expand her eyes as wide as can be, and sweetly ask, "May I have a cookie please?" No one could deny her.

By the time she was in grade school, she upped her game to knocking on neighbors' doors, claiming her starvation could only be sated with chips or chocolate. When she was six, the divorced single dad across the street who'd fed her once walked in on her rummaging through his fridge looking for more.

Sophie was a striking and beautiful creature, and quickly found the middle of the growth chart, averaging close to 50% for all measurements. During one checkup, the doctor told me that, technically, 50% was perfect.

"You didn't hear that," I said to Sophie.

"I totally heard that," she chuckled.

Sophie was all the more striking because of the contrast her looks brought to our family. Whereas Amara was physically dark, Sophie was light, blonde and blue-eyed until she was two, then her eyes shifted into a hazel of gold and green. But during those first years, she looked different from the rest of us.

By then, Blake was foreman at his job, so now and then, his crew would come by the house. One lunch hour, one of his guys—named Jack, of course, because every man I'd met during that era was named some form of Jack—took a gander at Sophie and pulled Blake aside.

"That little one is very blonde," he said in a hush.

"She sure is," Blake responded.

"But you aren't blond, and neither is your wife," Jack said. "And the older one doesn't have blonde hair either…"

"Jack, she's my kid," Blake sighed. "Genetics are complicated. Thank you for your concern, but I have not been made a cuckold."

Jack just blinked.

We didn't think much of it. After all, this was the same guy who, after finding out I had mono, told Blake that I must be cheating on him because it's a kissing disease.

Sophie was virtually speechless until she was a tad over two. When she still wasn't speaking at eighteen months, I got concerned. The doctor suggested we get her hearing tested.

She'd never had any ear infections, so we never paid much attention to her ears. When they tested her, they learned she was almost completely deaf, and probably had been for half her life. The doctor told me that to Sophie, the world sounded like it was emerged in water.

Blake was better about waiting for test results before getting worked up about anything, but immediately, I felt like a complete failure as a mother. How could I not know my child was deaf? Was there anything else I'd missed?

While trying to slow the wave of panic, I researched sign language lessons, but that left me feeling even more hopeless. I'm horribly deficient in areas of language. I simply lack the part of my brain that allows me to learn or speak anything other than basic English. I don't even try to pronounce foreign food names from menus; I just point and grunt. Despite these barriers, I was determined to master sign language if that's what I had to do to communicate with my daughter.

After talking with the doctor, the first step to fixing Sophie's hearing was to drain the excess fluid so they could see inside. They put her under sedation, and when it was over, the surgeon told me it was the thickest fluid he'd ever removed from anyone's ears. (Her deafness was so profound that they tested her brain at the same time, and thankfully, those tests came back fine.) Within three months of having her hearing restored through the draining process, Sophie was speaking well enough that she didn't qualify for speech therapy.

We'd go through cycles like this throughout her entire life. I'd find myself yelling at her, losing all of my patience, mad at her for blowing me off, and then I'd be like, oh yeah, she can't hear. My bad. So, we'd go back to the doctor and get her ears drained. She ended up getting three more sets of tubes, the last ones were done less than six months before she was murdered.

Sophie and Amara were polar opposites in how they responded to external validation. Amara was a "Look at me, Mom!" type, but Sophie didn't need anyone's approval.

When she was nine months old, I caught her walking on her own. I'd left her in the living room to grab something, and when I came back, I peeked around the corner at her. There Sophie was, walking towards the couch. Just going about her normal business, it seemed. I squealed with delight, and she looked at me and sat back down. I kept prodding her to show off this new skill, but she refused. Only when I stopped asking did she start walking on a regular basis.

This behavior continued throughout her life. When she came home from her first day of kindergarten, I asked where her folder was.

"That's my business," she said. "Not your business. You don't need to see anything."

Two years later, I got an email from her second-grade teacher telling me that Sophie had won a school district-wide art contest. She'd competed against hundreds of other kids and won! You'd think that would be something she'd want to share with her adoring mother, but when I asked her about it, Sophie's response was vague. "Oh that. I made one poster, lost it, and had to hurry up and make a replacement. The first one was much better." She never really cared what anyone else thought of her.

Parenting is a constant battle to transform an uncivilized heathen into a contributing member of society. When you're raising two children, that battle becomes a multi-front war. What works with one child inevitably fails with the next. I was constantly having to change my strategy to adapt to the demands of the most demanding child, whichever it may be. And I swear to the goddess that the only time they could get along with each other was when they joined forces to take me down.

By age three, Amara no longer napped. So whenever I tried to get Sophie down for a nap, I'd let Amara play in our backyard. After we'd moved in, we immediately fenced it in with the intended purpose of safely containing our offspring from imminent danger, and just as immediately, Amara began testing the fence like a velociraptor scanning for weaknesses. After a few failed attempts, I was confident she could be left unsupervised back there for at least twenty minutes.

But one day, while she was doing her round of perimeter tests, Amara saw a group of older kids playing one yard over. She called to them and politely requested they open the gate for her, since she couldn't reach it herself. It was only after I got Sophie settled in for her nap and went to check on Amara that I noticed the yard was completely empty and the back gate was open.

After a terrifying 15 minutes, I found her four houses down, playing on someone else's unguarded playset. She looked up at me with her big brown eyes and sighed. The gig was up and she knew it. Later, after I had finally calmed down and asked her if she understood how dangerous her behavior had been, she told me it was worth the punishment for the chance to play on such a cool playset.

Another time, Quinn had come to visit sporting an eye-catching toe ring that Amara instantly coveted. Amara went over to Quinn and slowly started rubbing her arm, gazing deeply into Quinn's eyes, as if she was trying to hypnotize her.

"Quinn, do you know what sharing is?" Amara quietly asked.

"Yes, that's when you give some of what you have to another person," Quinn explained.

"Sharing can also be when you give someone something for a few days and they give it back to you the next time they see you," Amara said.

Quinn said that was called "borrowing," and Amara went in for the kill.

"So then, I can borrow your toe ring?" Amara asked sweetly. "Because sharing is the nice thing to do."

The next few years with my girls went by in a blur. Our days had this cookie-cutter structure, filled with just enough embellishments to keep us sane. Diapers were changed and refilled. Meals were made, consumed, and cleaned up just in time for the next round. Billing and laundry cycles were infinity in motion, no end and no beginning. Sisyphus was my spirit animal.

When I first considered being a stay-at-home mom, I envisioned Martha Stewart-worthy activities and crafts. The reality was that I'd spend an hour prepping paper, glue, and paint for crafts that'd be blown through in ten minutes, and then another hour cleaning up the carnage. I'd be wiping the crumbs from the last snack just to hear a squeaky sweet voice declaring that she was starving, that didn't I have the decency to feed her once in a while? Simple outings to the zoo involved hours of strategic planning that never quite covered the bathroom emergency that would inevitably occur.

I battled entropy daily and found solace in surviving every hour still mostly sane. My contact with the outside world was limited to daily phone calls with my mother and best friend, Iris, and sharing barely-finished sentences with other moms at the playground.

Meanwhile, Blake, the only adult I'd see for days at a time, was a gamer. He simply wasn't present in reality, he was completely immersed in the fantasy world his video games existed in. My only option to connect with him was to join him.

Chapter Five

Video Games

During the day, I was Mom, Momma, or Mother, depending on the child. But at night, once the children where ensconced in their beds, I became FacetRed dwarf rogue, FacetBlue elf druid, or if I was feeling a little more devious, FacetBlack undead warlock.

It was 2005, and I'd dove helmet-first into a new reality. To infiltrate it, I had to create unique identities, learn a new language, and let the real world go for hours at a time.

Coming up with a screen name was easy. One of my favorite words had always been facetious and my favorite color is blue, but "facetiousblue" was just too damn long. So, I became "FacetBlue." When I needed to create more characters, I added more colors, and soon became "Facet[insert color of choice here]" to the masses that populated the imaginary land of *World of Warcraft*. Bet you didn't think a stay-at-home mom could be so, ahem, "multi-faceted."

While other players focused on slaughtering the undead or pillaging villages, my quest was more personal: find my missing husband.

Blake's daily routine was: wake up, go to work, get home, wade through the pile of small children trying to trap him with their affections, spend five hours in the bathroom on his SSS routine—that's "shit, shower, and shave," and okay, five hours may be an exaggeration.

But *I* never got the luxury of shitting, showering, or shaving in privacy while spending *all day* desperately awaiting his arrival, the only possible real human interaction I had. Children aren't quite human, as much as uncouth fairies, mad scientists, emotional tornadoes, not people to talk about current news or gossip with during the day. Finally, he would come out, shovel in a quick dinner, and migrate to the computer room. After six hours in there, he'd go to sleep, and do it all again the next day.

In retrospect, it's probably a telling statement that we never referred to the room where Blake would hole up as the "office." It was the "computer room." And no matter where we lived, we always had a place of prestige for that damn computer.

In our tiny apartment in Mankato, it was in our bedroom and it wasn't that big of a deal. The five months we lived there was the only time when the computer wasn't an issue, likely because it coincided with the era when Blake indulged his addiction while "studying" at the library or at his friend's place.

In our apartment in Minneapolis, the computer took over the space in this weird butlers' pantry between our kitchen and living room. It was nothing more than a slight widening of the short hallway, with a counter and just enough room for a chair, but he'd still squeeze in there to play his game for hours.

The third arrangement was in a basement bedroom of the Farmington house. It was basic: plain walls, cheap carpeting, lookout windows that allowed minimal natural light in. When we gutted it for renovations, his precious "girlfriend" moved into our bedroom. I hated having it in there. He'd stay up till the wee hours, and the glowing screen and clicking keyboard infested my dreams whenever I tried to snatch a few hours of sleep between middle-of-the-night feedings and diaper changes. Eventually, thankfully, she was reinstalled downstairs in the newly-finished room devoted entirely to her existence.

In the last home we shared—the big house in River Falls—the computer room was the second largest bedroom, down the hall from the master suite. This forced Cecilia into a tiny bedroom, while Amara and

Sophie shared the remaining room. The first thing I did when Blake and I split up was reclaim the bedrooms for their intended purpose and gave each of my daughters her own room.

As he moved his "girlfriend" from house to house, from room to bigger room, I attempted to understand the games themselves, mostly so I could hold a decent conversation with him. I spent some time playing *Diablo,* a game where your warrior character kills a bunch of monsters until, at the end, you kill the big monster. The way most video games are played, actually. These hesitant toe-dips into the gamer lifestyle worked fine enough until 2004.

I'd heard of *World of Warcraft* and thought the game would make a nice Christmas present for Blake, that in theory, I'd be buying him another game where you kill a bunch of monsters until you kill the big one.

Soon after he popped it in and logged on, I discovered I'd given my opiate-addicted husband the equivalent of pure heroin.

It's not accurate to describe *WoW* as a multiplayer online role-playing game. It's much more than that. It's a community and a lifestyle. It was *Dungeons and Dragons* on steroids.

The first step was creating an avatar. You picked its gender, race, allegiance, and class. You chose eye shape, nose size, hair style, and skin color. When your virtual identity was complete, you entered the world and made your way from low-level noob to epically-adorned raiding machine. Blake had five avatars he was serious about maintaining.

Another unforeseen aspect of the gift was that, unlike previous games he'd played, *WoW* never ends. Once you maxed it out to the highest possible level, the makers would inevitably release an expansion pack with more options, more levels, more worlds to explore. There was no final monster to beat, and this design devoured many a foolish young gamer. (Seriously, people played for so many hours that they literally died from starvation; look it up.) Blake's physical health was never at risk, but only because dirty looks from your wife can't literally hurt.

After *WoW* entered our lives, I barely saw Blake for the next four months. I began fantasizing about smashing the discs or deleting his account. I'd make snide remarks as he played.

"Your daughters think you've moved to a different country," I said one day.

"If you're looking for a divorce, you're on the right path." When I threatened to stop paying the monthly fee, that almost got his attention. Almost.

I felt like a complete idiot. I'd bought him the game without having any idea of its addictive powers. By the time I realized it, he was already long gone. I was used to coming in second place to his games, but with *WoW*, I wasn't even in the race. I felt helpless and lonely, with only myself to blame. Something had to give, and Blake wasn't the giving in type, so I adapted.

By that point, we'd been married almost five years, and I'd accepted it as a given that birthday presents from him would be nonexistent. That year, he and his brother, Cole, had a big surprise for me. They told me to close my eyes and led me by the hand into the computer room.

When I opened them, I saw a sleek black computer tower sitting next to a brand-new monitor. I didn't understand what I was looking at, and then Cole explained he'd built the computer from scratch, just for me. Blake even claimed it was slightly better than his.

And best, or worst, of all: they had *WoW* fully loaded and ready to go.

When I first got the gift, I saw the gesture as a gift from the man I loved wanting to spend time with me for the first time in years. What I didn't see was the truth: that it was a slick way for Blake to keep his marriage, as well as his video game habit, intact. Oblivious to this secret motive, I took a seat next to him and created a Dwarf Rogue to go adventuring along with his Dwarf Priest.

I spent almost three years playing *WoW* as various "Facet-" personas with Blake. They were probably the best years of our relationship.

Once, when the kids went away to their relatives, we spent an entire weekend playing *WoW*. Hour after hour, questing, taking down bosses, mastering levels, laughing at ridiculous storylines. We hadn't spent that much quality time alone together in years. He even talked to me more outside of the computer room. Sure, it was mostly game-related guild gossip, strategic planning to acquire epic gear, or ways to level-up our characters, but at least I was getting some interaction with him.

When you're ranked high enough, you have the ability to join a guild, and in doing so, have a community of like-minded people to chat with. We invested in headsets, so it was like being on a massive conference call when we played. This guild aspect was a big hook for me. I loved being a stay-at-home mom, but I'm also a very social creature, so it was great to get to know fellow guild members from all over the country, sometimes even around the world. We'd mostly chat about which mobs were dropping the best loot or strategies for beating an unbeatable boss, but occasionally threads about our real lives would seep in. While our characters obliterated zombies and giant lizards, we'd share antics about kids or pets (shockingly, most *WoW* players are single guys), or complain about irritating co-workers we wanted to use a banishing spell on.

I remember one particularly fun guild of unabashed nerds. One guy was a research scientist who spent his days working on drugs to battle AIDS, another lady was an IT worker for a large insurance company, and another was a construction man who built a female character because, as he put it, "If I'm going to spend hours staring at something, I want it to be a chick's ass." At times, the people in these guilds felt like my only real community.

But the relationships didn't last. Like any real-life relationships, there were fallings-out. It could stem from simple personality clashes, or from in-game fighting, like getting pissed off at someone for taking your loot, or for being dumb and causing your raiding party to die. It wasn't uncommon for Blake to get into ugly disagreements with fellow guild members, and when that happened, we'd both end up leaving the guild. When he'd inevitably get into another fight, I'd follow him to the next guild. And then the one after that. It was a never-ending cycle.

It wasn't a huge deal to me whenever we left. I was only half into the game anyway, but I could see how someone could totally lose themselves in this world. The allure is so so powerful. There was the entertainment of the game, the pull of checking-in with friends, and being able to be a member of a group without leaving the house or exposing your true self. Even now, years after I've quit *WoW* and severed all contacts to it, I still get nostalgic pangs for those fun days of endless questing and mythical adventuring.

But even back then, there was a limit to my investment. I was mindful about planning my time online, and treated going to the imaginary land like most people treat going away for the weekend.

Blake didn't have those same boundaries. I knew if I ever left him alone with the kids, he'd just sit them in front of a babysitting movie and log on. For the three years we played together, almost every "private date" involved spending our time in the computer room.

Once, on a rare occasion, we did venture out of the house together and it ended in complete disaster.

Blake's cousin, Beth, was getting married, and to celebrate, they had a joint bachelor/bachelorette party. All the girls were doing shots of tequila and invited me to join, not yet knowing that no good stories start with tequila.

Blake and I had a quick discussion and came to the understanding that if I did a shot, I wasn't driving home. He promised me that he'd stay sober, so I did that shot, then several more.

When I got to the point where I wanted to go home—you know, in the way a drunk decides the night is over and done *immediately*—he drove us back home.

We were less than a mile from the house when we saw the flashing lights from the cop car behind us. We pulled over, and Blake just barely blew the limit. When they took him to the station 30 minutes later, he was under again. Because of the "dewey" (that's what we call a DUI where I'm from), we had to pay out a ton in fines and fees, along with the hit on our insurance, and Blake lost the perk of having a work van for the next three years. But other than that, it didn't affect us too much. (Years later, he'd rewrite the story to make me the villain, claiming that I'd been completely sober and made him drive drunk just so I could lord it over him. This rewriting of history would become a regular occurrence.)

While we never explicitly talked about it, I assumed the role of sober cab driver after that incident. I couldn't trust him to keep us safe. I knew any agreement we had or promise that he made, would be forgotten the instant his whims changed. Blake was always going to do what Blake wanted to do, no matter the consequences to those around him.

Spring of 2006 found us at a crossroads. I'd taken full advantage of the questionable lending practices of the early 2000s, and my financial manipulations were coming to a head. I'd refinanced our original mortgage, and got an 80/20 mortgage with a five-year ARM, all a complex way of saying that we needed to either sell the house immediately for a profit or refinance it before the Adjustable Rate Mortgage expired. We decided to put the house on the market.

At the time, Blake and I were in a great place in our relationship emotionally. We'd found a balance that worked. I was happy spending my days with the kids and going on online quests with him at night. Since I wasn't working outside of the home, I felt all the household duties were my responsibility, and any bitterness I'd had over his lack of participation waned. We soon began weighing the pros and cons of another baby.

Three kids permanently pushed us into the world of minivans, and pulled me indefinitely out of the workforce. I loved having kids, and the horrors of my last pregnancy had faded far enough away. I was young and knew I'd have years ahead of me to get back into my career. Plus, I'd always liked driving a minivan. The pro that won out was a bit more morbid.

I've always been aware of how dangerous and complicated life can be, and I believe in a kind of nonsensical religion based on Murphy's Law. Let me give you an example. When I'm "on call" as a social worker,

I never indulge in alcohol. Not because I think a single glass of wine will incapacitate me, but because I'm convinced the literal act of pouring that glass will work its way through the universe and somehow create a call that I must respond to. It's similar to how I'm *absolutely positive* that getting a will done before I went on a recent cross-country trip kept the plane from crashing. (You're welcome, Delta Flight 1938.)

How did my superstition figure into our having a third child? I'd watched the bond form between Amara and Sophie, and had started thinking about the possibility that something tragic might happen to one of them, leaving the other to drift through life all alone. That idea was just too much for me. In my mind, having a third child would keep that from being a possibility, so I applied a bit of old school "an heir and a spare" family planning logic, and extrapolated that to cover siblings.

There Blake and I were, for the first time actually *choosing* to make a life. And like usual, almost as soon as we said "let's give it a shot," I was pregnant. Nine months later, we accepted congratulations in three different languages from our fellow *WoW* guild members. They were very understanding when I told them I needed maternity leave from the raiding crew.

Chapter Six

We're Going to Be Friends

I spent my first six years as a mother feeling like a cheat on the verge of being busted.

Every day, I waited for the maturity police to crash through my door and lock me away for committing Adult Fraud, and every night, I felt like I'd gotten away with the ruse for one more day. Maybe that paranoia was the result of becoming a mother at such a young age, or maybe it's a more universal response to being handed fragile creatures and being told "good luck and Godspeed" by society.

All I knew was that powerful entities were allowing me to buy and sell houses, make major medical decisions, and form the characters of two human beings while preparing to have a third.

In September of 2006, our house in Farmington, Minnesota was still up for sale, but we hadn't gotten any serious bites yet. The housing bubble was deflating, so we decided to take the house off the market. Of course, that's when we got an offer we couldn't refuse. The buyers wanted it for our asking price, the only stipulation being they also wanted to close in less than a month. We took the deal, and found our new home in a single weekend. We chose River Falls, Wisconsin.

Moving across the river to "the land of cheese and beer" cut Blake's commute to work in half. At that point, he was driving 45 minutes each way. Houses in River Falls were more affordable than the ones we were seeing closer to the Twin Cities. But more than that, when we visited the town itself, it just felt *right*. I wasn't a fan of hauling kids around the big city, and the suburbs lacked the boundaries and identity I craved. River Falls was that perfect midway point. All the charm of small-town living, but with a college nearby to keep it liberal enough for my edgy needs.

The real cincher was that Lennar, a major national builder, had started a new neighborhood with the spec house of my dreams. Everything inside was so new, shiny, and bursting with potential that we couldn't say no.

The main floor had a laundry room off the garage, a construction worker wife's dream come true, while the kitchen was large, open, and in the center like the beating heart of a home that it should be. There was a huge basement to be finished, feeding my dream that someday the girls would all get their own rooms, a master suite with a walk-in closet, and a fancy bathroom with an extra-large tub. All four bedrooms were on the same level upstairs, which was important to me and oddly difficult to find. And while the computer room would occupy one of the bedrooms, it'd be closer to the girls, so at night I could spend time with Blake while being accessible for night-time emergencies like bad dreams or empty sippy cups.

The home had everything I wanted, and best of all, it was being dumped due to the popping housing bubble. Not only was the price lowered to under what we were selling our home for, they also bought us points towards the mortgage. Which gave us a ridiculously low fixed rate we could not have gotten elsewhere. A few events had to be managed first before we moved in.

That year, my mom turned the big 6-0, and all she wanted was a special trip to Santa Fe with as little drama as possible. Louise and Rhett had rented a house for the five original Stouts to spend "quality time" together in, and the trip landed the week before we were set to move. No matter, Blake told me, he'd take care of the last of the packing while I was away.

"Enjoy puking in public places," he said as he sent me off.

The trip was great, full of bonding and laughter, despite all the public puking, and one night of horrid customer service. That one is worth a side-story, even if it starts like one of those angry Yelp! reviews.

My family is riddled with foodies. We love to eat, love to cook, and adore extravagant meals out. We've all done our time in the food service industry—my parents met because my father had wooed my mother with blueberry pancakes in the college cafeteria where they both worked—so, when I tell this story, understand that we all know what it's like to be a server.

One night in Santa Fe, we went to a tapas restaurant. It's a Spanish specialty that can best be summed up as lots and lots of appetizers. Every dish is about four bites of heavenly extravagant delicacies: prawns in sizzling chili oil, marinated unidentifiable vegetables, croquettes slathered in reduction sauces made from angel's tears of joy. But because of how it's all ordered and brought to the table, there's a rhythm to the meal that must be maintained. Our server, let's call him Dick, did not keep that rhythm.

He took our first order and left us stranded. When my water was empty, I was forced to stand up to beg him for a refill from across the room. When he saw me, he held up the pitcher, shrugged, and walked in the opposite direction. We ended up ordering only half the food we intended to because Dick didn't return to our table for intolerable stretches of time, so we left the restaurant completely unsatisfied.

As a result of all that, my brother left a single dollar tip on a several-hundred dollar tab. And Dick, who couldn't be bothered to fill a pregnant lady's glass when she was desperately thirsty, somehow found the energy and time to chase us into the parking lot for a stern talking-to.

My brother was the first out the door, way ahead of the rest of us. I was waddling at the tail end. (Yes, when it's your third pregnancy, you waddle well before your first trimester is over.) That put me in a position to be the first one to hear Dick yelling profanities at my brother. And when I did, immediately, without hesitation, I spun on a dime right in his face. I was too angry to speak, but apparently my glare was enough to convey my emotional state. Dick took one look at me and ran back into the restaurant.

But I wasn't satisfied.

I waddle-chased him back into the kitchen, tearing into him the whole time while steadying my baby belly.

"You have the gall to follow us out to the parking lot when you couldn't be bothered to actually wait on our table!" I shouted. "You better hide, you coward!"

Dick wisely ducked behind his manager, a very intelligent woman whose motivation was to avoid a lawsuit, and stayed hidden behind her for my entire tirade. "Ma'am, you have every right to be angry," the manager said, and refunded the meal while staring daggers at Dick.

By that point, Jack had run back into the restaurant. He wanted to protect his baby sister, especially while she was in the process of carrying another niece. When he found out that it was Dick who needed the protection, he was blown away. My poor brother probably felt like he'd stepped into an alternate universe. Jack, who's always had the rage while I've been the Zen master, had to calm *me* down. Total role reversal.

After that excitement, we wrapped up our trip and headed back to our various homes throughout the Midwest.

I arrived in Minnesota the day before we moved, and, of course, Blake hadn't done any of the packing he'd promised. When our friends and family arrived to load the U-Haul, our dishes and clothes were still in the drawers and cupboards. One practical friend took the initiative to pack the dishes with my clothes, while I did my best to frantically shove the toiletries and toys in whatever boxes I could find. When I unpacked on the other side of the river, I found underwear nestled between plates, bras wrapped around coffee mugs, and silverware shoved into socks.

Despite the last-minute chaos, our family moved with hopes of a future that seemed to be only getting brighter.

Amara, then six years old, staked her claim to some personal space in a bedroom immediately, and had her stuff unpacked before the moving truck stopped rolling. Then, she ran around the neighborhood looking for friends. She came back home disappointed when she found out that most of the lots were vacant, the homes yet to be sold. I pointed out the untamed lot behind our house was sure to be filled with wildlife, and her dismay was alleviated some.

The first time we watched out of our back windows, a bald eagle swooped down and carried off a rodent. We were amazed. It was like living in an episode of *Planet Earth*. The next time it happened, we were outside, and got a better perspective of just how enormous these carnivores were.

Amara turned to me. "Did you know eagles can carry off small dogs?" she asked.

I looked at my petite child, who'd fallen off the growth charts by her fourth month of life and was yet to get back on them.

"Amara, do you realize you aren't much bigger than a small dog?"

"Duly noted, Mom," she simply stated. "I will take necessary precautions."

In my mind, 2006 was the year Amara stopped being my baby and started becoming the main source of my frustration and guilt. This was the year when if I said "right," she insisted "left." No matter what I said or did, I was wrong, and my ability to please her diminished to nothing, a feeling that soon became mutual. This was the era when I began using such wonderfully clichéd phrases like, "You are old enough to know better," "Why do you have to make every simple task so difficult?" and my soon-to-be-classic retort, "Actually, Amara, I do know what I'm talking about!"

The age-old battle between mothers and their oldest daughters played out between us daily. We had long, one-sided conversations about what it meant to be grateful and appreciative of what you have in life, others where she turned the tables and lectured me about the merits of her fresh ideas versus my tired old propaganda. The punk in me wilted under the blaring realization that I had become The Man.

"Actually, Mom…" she'd start.

(She had this habit of obnoxiously starting conversations with "actually" that would instantly irritate me, but now I crave her condescension desperately.)

"…it's far more efficient to organize my books by genre than by size."

"Actually, Amara," I said, always responding before I could check my impatience, "it *is* far more efficient to just listen to me the first time and pick up your room instead of initiating a debate about shelving practices!"

This was also the year Amara broke my toe, or to be more technically accurate, I broke my toe *on* Amara.

The carpet guys were at the house, so I took the kids to the corner coffee shop to play. As I was bent into the van, trying to unbuckle my two-year-old Sophie out of her seat, Amara decided the best use of her time would be to run around me, ducking and swaying to avoid any direct contact. I was wearing sandals, so when I stepped to escape this virtual pen she had me in, her heavily armored tennis shoe collided with my exposed toes. The pain was unbearable, and I'm still shocked I didn't drop Sophie. Both girls learned several new swear words in that moment, though. It was the first time in my life I'd ever broken a bone and I was shocked that there was nothing to do for it but ride it out. Like a lot of things in life, it hurt like hell, but I just had to carry on.

The epitome of my bad parenting that year, however, came when Amara took advantage of a moment of distraction and played "beauty shop."

I'd been providing daycare for a neighbor, and had left the kids playing in Amara's room while I cleaned up the lunch dishes. I was only gone a few minutes, but when I returned, I noticed Amara had cut a chunk out of her sister's hair, a chunk from her friend's hair, and even managed to mutilate her own. Amara's was so badly butchered we had to shave her head to even it out. When we cleaned her up, she looked just like me when I'd first gotten pregnant with her.

The bad parenting part wasn't being distracted long enough for these hijinks to occur. That happens to the best of us. It was my response to it.

After we shaved her head, I was worried the other kids in preschool might make fun of her with this new look. So, the night before she went back in, I tried talking to her about how some of the kids might laugh at her, maybe think her new hairdo was funny.

"Not very many girls have super short hair like this," I explained to her. "I mean, you really butchered your hair, honey! It's such a drastic change from how they last saw you that you should expect them to be shocked."

I was trying to be loving, but instead, I planted seeds of neurosis, and basically gave her an anxiety attack. She worried about it so much overnight, that the next day, she began crying before she went off to school. And worse of all, my preparations were completely unnecessary. Most of the kids didn't even notice, and those that did, thought her haircut was cool as hell.

Shortly after this incident, Amara got sucked under the treadmill.

I had assumed it was safe to zone out and burn some calories since the toddler was napping, and my almost six-year-old was playing quietly like she did most afternoons. But behind me, Amara, my constant scientist, was holding a large plastic ball against the back of the treadmill, watching it spin in her hands. She was learning about the Magnus effect, but got a lesson in pain instead.

The ball got sucked under the treadmill, and Amara went with it. She was covered in friction burns on her neck, face, and arms. If she hadn't chopped off her long hair, it would've likely have been way worse.

In that moment, I officially forfeited any claims to being a calm, rational mother who's good during a crisis. My first response was to yell at her, the treadmill, the ball, and myself. I was terrified I'd do something to further injure her, so I gave Amara some Tylenol and sat with her until someone more detached could help.

I called Blake in a state of complete hysteria, and he left work immediately to clean her wounds and bandage her up. While Blake calmly and systematically debrided her scrapes and applied a thin layer of ointment, I scrubbed the layer of her skin off the treadmill. With her shaved head and bandaged arms, she was a walking testament to my fine parenting.

Amara was fantastic about starting kindergarten and switching to a new school after six weeks, while I was neurotic. I cried at the thought of her getting on a school bus. During this emotional and hormone-ravaged time, I managed to handle just one of Amara's life events like a real honest-to-goodness grown-up.

Pretty much my entire family is nearly blind, so it wasn't surprising when, during a regular check-up, Amara was diagnosed with an astigmatism and chronic farsightedness. When she got glasses, I let her pick out the frames, insisting everyone would think they were as cool as she did. Secretly, I was somewhat worried that between the super-thick red frames and her insistence on wearing her pants hiked up to her chest, she'd be mocked. Any kid looking like that growing up in my era would've been made fun of relentlessly, but I was wrong again. The kid had style!

Amara loved her teacher, and thought school was the bee's knees. On one of the first days at her new kindergarten, her teacher asked her what her favorite book was, and Amara told her, "I prefer nonfiction. My favorite book is *What's Out There* by Stephen Hawking."

Amara also met Jade, a young girl who'd become her BFF. Jade's mom, Dawn, and I became great friends, and we still are. Dawn was the one who held me the day I learned my girls were murdered.

Amara and Jade were a great match. They loved playing wolves together, having sleepovers, and even working on school projects. Jade was the reason Amara found soccer and Amara was the one reason Jade didn't hate school for the longest time. They truly balanced each other like yin and yang strongest in the middle where they came together.

Sophie, Sophie, oh my dear Sophie.

The year between a child's second birthday and their third is difficult because they slowly morph from an easily-forgivable baby to a willfully disobedient tyrant. Amara was always a very logical and verbal fighter, while Sophie established herself as pure emotional, expressing her feelings with passionate, often physical force. Sophie spent most nights that year waking me up at least once in the middle of the night, but I beamed with pride at the end of the year when she'd finally stopped biting people.

Like Amara, Sophie took disobedience to a whole new level. Her main response to being told to pick up her toys, or wash her hands, or stop destroying the few nice things we owned was blinking her eyes and asking "what?" while doing the opposite of whatever she'd been told. Fortunately, she balanced these negative attributes by becoming very polite and acquiring some endearing traits, always saying "please" and "thank you very much!"

The best example of her Jekyll/Hyde personality was her tantrum over the coveted family copy of *Chicka Chicka Boom Boom*. One day, we were in the family room reading books, playing with toys, and just hanging out. At some point, Sophie lost interest in the toys in front of her, and eyed her sister, who was contentedly perusing a book. Like most two-year-olds, her desire went from 0-60 in about three breaths.

"I want that book!" she blurted out.

"I'm reading it, get a different one," Amara reasonably responded.

Sophie began to wail at the top of her lungs and screeched, "Give me the book!" over and over like a siren.

As soon as Amara gave in to her request, the waterworks stopped. Sophie calmly said, "Thank you very much for the book, Amara," like they'd just had the most polite and civilized exchange.

Amara and I locked eyes and sighed, like we were members of a bomb squad that had just survived another potential explosion.

Sophie was extremely affectionate. Lots of hugging, kissing, cuddling, and oodles of nuzzles. She'd often grab my face with both of her pudgy little hands, stare deeply into my eyes, and plant a long, wet, occasionally snotty kiss on my lips until I turned blue and gasped for air.

It was during this developmental stage that Sophie also found her inner advocate.

Often, Amara would make Sophie cry. It was almost a daily occurrence. Whenever I walked in to find out what had happened, I'd ask Amara what she did, and her responses ranged from "nothing, well, nothing that justifies crying like that" to "I took my toys back, because they're mine, and she just messes them up."

I'd lecture her and formulate repercussions for her actions, but before I could get out her penalty, Sophie would stand between us, shoving me away.

"She's my friend," she'd plead.

Of course, it worked. How could anyone not be calmed down by that?

Managing a baby is easier than a toddler, because with a baby, whenever they do something wrong, you can always add on the handy mental caveat of, "oh, she doesn't understand what she's doing." At some point, that goes away, or at least, it should. I likely kept Sophie in my mind as a baby longer than I should have, and boy, did I pay for it later.

Throughout that year, Sophie became very clingy, especially once we moved to Wisconsin, when it was just the two of us in the house most of the time. Our relationship became very codependent. From the moment she woke until the second she slept, she was within two feet of me. This meant I often resorted to letting her have her way, just to get some peace, which was a problem because, most often, all she wanted was me.

This occasionally manifested in hilarious ways. Sometimes, if I wasn't paying enough attention to her, if I needed a moment's rest as I carried another being within me, Sophie would shove a stuffed animal up her shirt, lie on the couch with an arm draped over her eyes, and moan, "I'm so sick! I have baby in my tummy, and I'm so sick!" Then, she'd roll over and pretend to puke. Her mocking me in my misery was the birth of her wicked sense of humor that I couldn't resist laughing at—even when I was the object of her jokes. Other family members were not able to roll with her personality as smoothly as Amara and I did.

Blake, on the other hand, wasn't around much and was never a real hands-on parent. He'd give them sprinkles of attention as he passed through the house on his way for a cigarette or to the computer room. So, it came as no surprise that Sophie was not as inclined to accept ministrations from him when I *could* get him to help out.

One night, I asked Blake for help getting Sophie ready for bed. Now, two-year-olds require a bit of finesse in every interaction. They're like ticking bombs that have three different triggers, and one of them is always hidden. It didn't take much for Blake to set her off, and once she was in full-blown fit mode, all he did was put her in a time out and went about his normal business. Meanwhile, I was left to deal with the tantrum and get the kids ready for bed myself.

My resentment built to the point where it was no longer concealable, so, after making sure the kids were asleep, I walked into the computer room and interrupted him during his game time.

"You set her off on purpose so you wouldn't have to do the work of actually getting her ready for bed!" I said.

This led into a tirade of me dressing him down for never helping, for basically being little more than a paycheck and a warm body in the home. I don't recall all the details, but I do remember that the argument became physical, for the first time in our marriage. He grabbed me by my arms, picked me up, shook me, then pushed me towards our bed. He almost hit me in the face, but he stopped himself. He walked away, and I let him.

The next day, I had a large ugly bruise on my left arm. When we had a quiet moment, I told him I could cover this up, but if he ever hit me in the face, I wouldn't be able to make excuses. It was a long time after that before I tried to get him to be more involved with the kids' care.

I'd thought that not having to go to work every day would magically make the horrors of pregnancy easier, but that wasn't true. I woke up wanting to vomit, and the feeling never left until I was unconscious. I took medication to help me through the first trimester, but it eventually gave me migraines. Puking in my kitchen sink because I was too big to bend over a toilet was a joy, and this time around, I had the added bonus of round ligament pain. Basically, it felt like someone had beaten me with a baseball bat in every part of my body that was, let's say, the area where a saddle would touch. It didn't abate until I gave birth, at which point, it magically disappeared.

During those nine long months, I knew I'd never have to go through this process again. This was to be the last one. After this, I was done making people!

We decided Blake should be the one to get snipped for practical reasons—money, time, and childcare the most dominant among them. A vasectomy took 15 minutes and cost a quarter of what a tubal costs, which also involves being put under anesthesia and spending hours in the hospital, versus a recovery process that necessitated a bag of frozen peas and hours of gaming. So, before Cecilia made her debut, we shut down the baby factory for good.

I found a church that fit my odd set of beliefs. I wanted a spiritual aspect in the girls' lives, and also felt the need to have some connection to my surroundings. In Farmington, I'd tried a Lutheran church, but the sermons didn't jive with me. After we moved to River Falls, I went online to take a quiz called "Belief-O-Matic," and it spit out I was either a Unitarian or Quaker.

So, I searched for Unitarian churches, and the girls and I tried a few services before becoming official members. I joined a women's circle that met once a month, and shortly before Cecilia was due to be born, they held a "birthing way" for me. It's kind of a ritual of wishing well on the new child. It was nice.

For the first time, I felt like I was part of a community, and more prepared than ever to let the munchkin growing in my belly bust out.

Cecilia was due to arrive on May 15th, but that day came and went with nothing. In the early morning hours of the 16th, I started to get contractions and told Blake that he shouldn't bother going into work. He turned off his alarm and went back to sleep.

I woke up and went about my day like usual: sent Amara off to school, fought with Sophie to eat something with more sustenance than a bite of cereal, and got the house in order. Finally, we were off to the small, local hospital about a mile from home.

Most of Cecilia's birth is clouded in my memory. I remember that Cole, Blake's brother, and Raya, his future wife, showed up just in time for the shit to get real. I think Amara had just gotten off the school bus as Blake and I were headed to the hospital.

I remember the doctor breaking my water, and somehow catching everything in a large bucket, which impressed me at the time. So neat and tidy! I also recall that when the nurse checked to see how dilated I was, her hand and half her arm became trapped in my vagina during a contraction. We chatted for a bit until it passed, easily the most awkward conversation I've ever had.

I can't tell you how long I pushed for, or what time Cecilia was actually born. It's all foggy now. Blake was there for the whole labor and delivery, but if I try to focus on one particular moment with him, it blurs into a mix of scenes from all three births, like a film negative layered one on top of another. I *do* remember I didn't even think about holding off on an epidural this time.

When Cecilia Lee was born, they placed her immediately onto my bare chest, and I swear that in that moment, my heart exploded from my ribcage and enveloped her. She was my last baby, and I was going to soak up every drop of squishy babyness I could.

The girls came to meet her twelve hours after her escape. Amara ran in sporting freshly broken glasses that had been taped together in the middle. I asked her what happened.

"I applied pressure to them until they cracked down the middle," she explained in true Amara fashion. And for the life of me, I couldn't understand what she was talking about. She took a deep breath, sighed dramatically, and demonstrated that she'd used both hands on either side to push them up her nose.

"Like this, Mom!" she said. "And, obviously, I applied too much pressure."

The matter closed, she went back to cooing at Cecilia.

Sophie was a little less impressed with the squirming bundle being hoisted onto her lap. After a perfunctory once-over, she announced, "I guess she is kinda cute," and that was that.

Blake went home almost immediately to catch up on sleep and regain a bit of humanity via a hot shower. The next day was full of visitors, and on the 18th, we all went back home together to figure out how to be a family of five.

Flash forward seven years later. The house would be demolished, and in its neighborhood space would be nothing but an empty lot.

Chapter Seven

Cecilia

I've always enjoyed listening to the Simon & Garfunkel song "Cecilia." The refrain is catchy, the melody is infectious, and the lyrics a tad naughty. I remember hearing it on the radio as a small child and realizing for the first time that a song could make me feel joyous and full of light all at the same time. Since then, I'd wanted to give a daughter that name. But when I was twenty-one and pregnant with daughter number one, I lacked the confidence needed to defend some of the more scandalous lyrics in the song.

So, Amara became Amara. When I was twenty-four with daughter number two, I still lacked the confidence, and so Sophie became Sophie. But at twenty-eight, with daughter number three on her way, I no longer had the same qualms. Plus, we had a matter of urgency to deal with.

"She has to have a name before the girls meet her, or they'll name her!" I told Blake from the hospital bed, cradling our hours-old, nameless baby girl. I had good reason to be concerned.

Sophie, you see, had been spending the last three months telling everyone I was gestating her purple baby sister.

"I did *not* spend the last nine months puking so I can raise a daughter named Purple!" I said to him.

Amara, meanwhile, had dreams of naming her Serafina after her go-to name when playing "make believe." Not as bad as Purple, but it still didn't fly with me, so we made it official before they got the chance.

On May 17ᵗʰ, 2007, I yelled several names to Blake as a way of practicing what her name sounded like, and "Cecilia Lee" was the one that stuck.

My favorite memory of Cecilia and her melodic namesake was her baby dedication at our very liberal Unitarian Universalist church.

When it came to religious activities, I ran the show and Blake, who was indifferent to religious beliefs or spirituality, occasionally tagged along for big events. To call Blake an atheist would be implying that he cared enough to have an opinion. He loved antagonizing his devout siblings and would often say things to rile them up. But at the bottom of his consciousness, he didn't believe in anything beyond his immediate reality.

I, on the other hand, have always valued all beliefs and spirituality. I had a very eclectic religious upbringing. My maternal grandmother was raised devout Christian Scientist, my mother was raised Easter/Christmas Presbyterian, and my father came from Missouri Synod Lutherans. When I was a kid, summers were spent bouncing from bible school to bible school in western Pennsylvania, so there was a lot of exposure to Wesleyan Methodists, who were like Amish devotees but with electricity and cars. During high school, one of my BFFs was Orthodox Jewish, so I spent a lot of time with that sect, followed by years with hardcore Catholics.

On my own, I dug a bit into Buddhism, Hinduism, Native American, Pagan, plus a touch of Islam. I've always felt like I was a part of many communities, and appreciated the threads that religion can connect us through. And I love a good ritual.

After I became a mother, I wanted my babies welcomed into the community of souls that inhabit our planet. I wanted them blessed, loved, and acknowledged. It took me a long time to find a church that fit, so while I was searching, I used my parent's church to meet my religious needs.

We had Amara and Sophie baptized in their Lutheran church in Springfield, Illinois when they were babies, the same church where Blake and I were married. When Cecilia joined us, I jumped at the chance to have her dedicated at the Unitarian Universalist Society.

Instead of scripture, I read Kahlil Gibran's passage "On Children." It starts like this:

> *Your children are not your children.*
>
> *They are the sons and daughters of Life's longing for itself.*
>
> *They come through you but not from you,*
>
> *And though they are with you, yet they belong not to you.*

Cecilia was sprinkled with daisy water instead of holy water, and was dedicated to the entire world instead of just one of its religions. At the end of the ceremony, instead of a traditional hymn in her honor, we sang Simon & Garfunkel's song. The entire congregation, from ninety-year-old grandmas to babbling toddlers, unabashedly belted out every lyric. It brought tears to my eyes.

Unfortunately, that song haunted Cecilia for the five years she was with us, and whenever I hear it now, years after her death, I feel like her spirit is reaching out to me.

Amara and Sophie would nail the beginning of the song in perfect chorus, before their frustration boiled over into their own unique rendition. "Now won't you please stop crying / because you're breaking my ears!"

This was the soundtrack to our home in 2007.

Little Cecilia looked nothing like either of her sisters, but rather a perfect mix of the two, like the equator between polar opposites. She was to be my last baby, snipping Blake's tubes made sure of that, and so I wanted her babyhood to drag on forever. Cecilia soon scoffed at that plan.

What I'm about to describe flies in the face of scientific norms, like an alien abduction or a dog that can juggle, but I have witnesses, even video proof. I am not lying, nor exaggerating in the slightest. Cecilia Lee was walking by the time she was seven months old. It was like Cecilia saw her two older sisters running around, and was like, "fuck this rollin'-around shit, I gotta get moving!" This would become a common theme throughout her short life.

She crawled and pulled herself to stand before most babies rolled over. She climbed chairs at eight months, and on her first birthday, after I put her down for a nap in a pack-n-play (think: crib with mesh siding), when I went back to get her, she'd climbed to the nearby top bunk and was reaching for the ceiling fan. It was ridiculous and creepy. She looked like your average baby, but moved like a toddler, and kept me on my toes for damn sure. She spent her entire life proving she was just as capable as Amara and Sophie when it came to getting into mischief and obliterating expectations.

"Cecilia" was hard for three-year-old Sophie to fully enunciate, so she quickly shortened it to "Cea." This came in handy when Sophie would loudly complain about Cea multiple times a day.

"Cea smells gross. Is that poop? Disgusting."

"Why is Cea eating your boob? How much longer do I have to wait? Just put her down."

"All she does is cry!"

"Cea is wearing my favorite shirt! She is getting her cooties all over it."

"STOP stealing my stuff!"

When she was teeny-tiny, Cea's primary offenses were sucking up my time and attention from Sophie. As she got bigger, so did the crimes. Sophie had zero tolerance for a snoopy kid sister who touched her precious things, and then had the gall to wear her hand-me-down clothes. When the girls were a few years older, Sophie scarred her Aunt Milly and Uncle Jack who were not yet parents by announcing in a very calm and thought-out manner, "I really wish my sisters were dead," she said. "Even better yet, I wish they had never been born. It would be so nice to be the only one."

No matter how vociferous Sophie was about the pains her baby sister caused, she'd be the first on the scene to comfort the tyke.

If Cea had an owie, Sophie was the first to plant a kiss on it. If Cea was frustrated with life, Sophie was working to make her giggle to forget her woes. When Cecilia established herself as a bed hopper, Sophie would loudly declare every night before bed, "Tonight Cea, you will not sleep with me!" But just as often, in the middle of the night, I'd find Sophie had changed beds to sleep with Cea because she'd begged her to cuddle.

One would think a six-year-old would be more capable of keeping an eye on an infant than a three-year-old, but that wasn't the case with Amara.

Amara would constantly be lost in a project or book, and whenever she was, the rest of the world might as well have disappeared. I'd occasionally dare to indulge in bodily functions, like using the restroom or taking a shower, leaving Cecilia under Amara's care. When I'd get back, the little one would be crying in frustration, begging for nothing more than an acknowledgement, but Amara was too focused on building a robot or reading a book to register the noise, let alone address the wails.

Sophie, on the other hand, waited for Cea to mew a bit before yelling, "Mom, Mom, MOM! The baby needs you!" And then she'd pat her baby sister on the tummy and whisper, "It's okay, baby, she'll show up eventually."

I'm not sure if it was nature, nurture, or simply a shift in my perspective, but Cea was my easiest baby. Gone was the nervousness and fear of the unknown that had plagued those first years of child-rearing. Obliterated were the idealistic fantasies of cherubic children and a life of Martha Stewart moments. All that was left was a fathomless appreciation for the weight of a new soul's gaze, and the undeniable connection between us. Cea and I just found our groove together right from her first breath to her last.

While Cecilia's thread blended into our family tapestry smoothly, the weave of Blake's career began to unravel. The year 2007 destroyed many of our assumptions and plans. This was the start of the slow death of

Blakes's career, when the small cracks in what had been a solid foundation began to appear.

The framing company where Blake had worked began to feel the pinch of the housing market crash. Changes were made to stave off impending devastation, including changing how vacation checks were doled out, from a single bonus at the beginning of the year if days weren't used, to the more classic "use it or lose it" method. This was a big deal to Blake, who never took vacation time.

Forced to use them or get nothing, he took off the week following Cecilia's birth. I tricked myself into thinking he was taking time off to provide support during my recovery, maybe with some grocery shopping or a little cleaning, but no. This was *his* vacation, so he spent the time like one. The only difference: instead of going to some beachside resort, he holed himself up in the computer room and took an all-expenses paid trip to game world.

Blake's company tried to adapt to the changing economy in other ways, too, including hiring a consulting company to help them become more "efficient." Whenever a new crew of suits shuffled into an office meeting, Blake would come home and gripe.

"They're throwing away thousands of dollars listening to idiots who throw fish around," he said one day, "instead of just looking at the numbers to see who gets the job done!"

Blake always had the best or second-best rates in the company, and was used to getting regular raises and kudos for his hard work. When the company tightened finances, these perks disappeared. Being "the best" suddenly wasn't as lucrative or ego-building as it had been, and more concerning, the jobs he had to take were getting further and further away from home. We'd moved to River Falls to be closer to work, and now he had to drive sixty miles through and around the Twin Cities twice daily.

One of the final disasters for Blake's job, and thusly our way of life, was when the company created a "safety inspector" position and filled it with someone Blake had never been able to tolerate. Let's call him SHA, for "Sue Happy Antagonist."

After he was given this role, SHA would show up to Blake's work sites weekly, ostensibly to "examine safety," but really just disrupted the crew. After several months, Blake's tolerance for this arrangement dwindled to nothing.

One day, at the end of the long, hot summer, SHA came to the site and gathered the crew in a framed-in room on the second floor of a house in mid-build. After a bit, Blake had noticed no one was working, found them all in the room, and told everyone to get back to work. Blake and SHA exchanged some terse words. In the middle of the conversation, Blake grabbed a three-ring-binder full of info SHA had been collecting, and tossed it out the window. It landed on a part of the roof, and SHA climbed out to retrieve the binder, and then jumped back into the room.

Recollections differ regarding what happened next.

SHA claimed Blake grabbed his neck. Blake said he put his hands up to keep SHA from knocking him over as he jumped into the room. In either case, SHA walked away, and Blake thought nothing of it. Then, the police arrived.

Cell phone records showed that SHA went to his truck, called his lawyer, then called the police, saying that Blake had choked and assaulted him. When the police showed up, they asked Blake if he had touched SHA, and he said "yes," but didn't describe anything. Blake wasn't arrested or booked, but charged with a misdemeanor, which he figured out when he got the court summons in the mail a few weeks later. At that point, finally, when it was already a full-blown crisis, Blake told me about the whole ordeal.

"It didn't seem worth mentioning at the time," he said when I questioned him about why he kept me in the dark so long. "It was just so ridiculous."

He began talking to some people at work and discovered that SHA had at least three active lawsuits against other employees and the company itself. It meant that the company couldn't give Blake any legal resources. They told him he better get a lawyer, and a good one, because if the charge wasn't thrown out, SHA would sue him civilly for injuries.

I'd always managed our finances, so it was on me to hire the lawyer. I reached out to friends and family and got the names of two. One had a price tag of $4,500, which we couldn't afford, and the other cost a more reasonable $1,200. We sat down in the kitchen to go over our options.

I felt like the pricey lawyer was overkill for the situation we were in, and sincerely had faith that justice would be on our side. Either way, we simply couldn't afford to pay that much money for his defense.

Blake had harbored a general resentment of the legal system dating back to his years of juvenile delinquency, when he felt he'd suffered harsher consequences than he should have because he never had enough legal support.

"If my parents had gotten me a lawyer or stood up for me," he told me, "I wouldn't have had to spend weekends in jail as a kid."

I tried to tell him this was different, that back then he *had* been guilty of what he was accused of, that the fact he'd broken laws and didn't get away with it wasn't a sign of a world against him. But it didn't make a dent. Blake told me that if I didn't get him the best lawyer, and if this charge didn't go away, he'd hold me personally responsible for the financial ruin that the civil lawsuit would bring upon our home. He said he'd never forgive me for not backing him up.

What could I do? He was my husband, he was scared, and he needed me to prove I believed in him. But I was no magician. I couldn't create money out of thin air. So, I ate my pride, and went on my hands and knees to my brother for a loan. He paid for the fancy lawyer, and the case was dismissed at the first hearing because someone finally thought to interview the witnesses. Guess that's why you pay the big bucks.

Even with the dismissal, that shitshow finally pushed Blake to jump ship.

Late in the fall, he had begun talking to his old foreman, Hank, who had both an entrepreneurial spirit, and more importantly, a high-earning spouse. It was enough for Hank to go into business for himself. For the past couple of years, he'd been going from job to job, switching up the makeup of his crew as needed. It worked for Hank, because he didn't need the trappings of a big company while his wife's job provided benefits and a fall-back income.

At some point, he invited Blake to work on his next project. I wasn't wild about the idea, but my need for stability was trampled by Blake's need to be his own boss. However, working on an independent crew was a different experience than Blake was used to.

When he worked for the construction company, he was paid a regular hourly rate plus overtime. He clocked his hours and got a nice fat check at the end. Working with Hank meant bidding for a job, getting a big chunk of money, and that was it. If they got the job done for the number of hours they bid, they were golden. If the job took longer—and the first one did—they were screwed. Blake figured out the exact hour that he started making less money, and began to obsess about the exact minute he began working for free.

Once that first house was framed, Hank moved onto the next job and Blake declined to go with him. He knew he didn't have what it took to roll with the punches of freelancing, but Blake also couldn't bring himself to go back to the construction company, either. I still don't know what he was thinking or feeling, I just know what he did. Or, more accurately, what he didn't do.

He stopped working.

I finally asked him when his next job would start. When he simply answered that he didn't "have one to start," I freaked out. I lost my mind. I became nothing more than a mass of cells quivering in fear. All I knew was that he was now home all the time, absolutely no help to me, and oh yeah, we had no money coming in. Something had to give.

He applied to work for some other big companies like the construction company, but they were either union or not hiring because of the work slowdown. We poured over our finances together, trying to figure out what options we had. The house was our biggest expense, but also our biggest piggy bank. Blake became fixated on getting our equity out of it. I was skeptical, but told him we could look into it.

A realtor came in and was optimistic about selling it quickly.

The realization that we had nothing tying us to the place was freeing. We could move anywhere, find a new job in a new place. Maybe that would bring back Blake's drive and restore our family's structure.

Instead, I made what I consider one of the biggest mistakes of my life.

I ran home to Mama.

Chapter Eight

Mama, I'm Coming Home

Blake needed a job.

After searching for a few weeks, he couldn't find one he was willing to do, and so, with nothing keeping us in River Falls except a big-ass house and a little history, it was time to get out.

Running away felt right. When I'd first moved north to the frozen wastelands of Minnesota and Wisconsin, I had no intention of making it a permanent lifestyle. I was supposed to get my degree, move back to Springfield, marry my hometown boyfriend, and live happily ever after. But then I got knocked up, and one thing led to another, which led to damn near a decade of northern exposure. Returning to Springfield was a chance to recapture some of those lost dreams.

Meanwhile, my more "logical" justifications for a move back went like so: the house would sell faster if we weren't living in it; the cost of living in Springfield was much lower than in River Falls; and my best friend Iris still lived there, so we'd be able to raise our kids together like we'd always wanted. We couldn't afford two house payments, but that was no problem. My parents lived in a huge house, and my mom had long clamored about wanting us to move back so they wouldn't have to travel as far to see her grandchildren. We could easily make living together work for a couple months, right?

More importantly, Mom knew lots of people down in Springfield. Some of them ran businesses, and therefore, needed employees. One person she knew owned a small window replacement company, and he told her he'd have plenty of work for Blake once we arrived. This message was passed along to Blake, who scheduled a phone call with his potential new boss.

After the call, I remember Blake having qualms about the conversation. I pressed for details.

"I don't know, babe," he said. "It was just odd. He didn't want to talk about anything in detail until I came in person."

I shut down these hesitations with the blunt hammer of denial.

"If my mom says you have a job, you have a job," I told him. "She'd never let us move without a source of income."

Everything was quickly put in motion. I'd given notice to the family that I provided daycare for, arranged for the kids to switch schools, booked the moving truck, put a deposit down on a storage unit in Springfield, and my parents, Rhett and Louise, started prepping for our arrival.

In early March of 2008, the five of us packed up everything we owned in a U-Haul, bid farewell to our friends and family in River Falls, and headed south to the eager embraces of our friends and family in Springfield.

And so began the worst ten months of my life before my children were murdered.

At the time, my parents were living in a large, four-bedroom house, complete with an enormous backyard perfectly designed for the enjoyment of growing children. They'd been living there the past six years, upsizing after years in a three-bedroom townhouse in order to accommodate my mom's new home daycare business. Before we arrived, she'd closed that business to do taxes and bookkeeping full time, a jolt to her system that she was still adjusting to.

Meanwhile, my dad had been grinding out his last few years as a traveling salesman for a farm equipment company. He'd been there for

18 years, and the last several were the most difficult. The company had changed his territory to the deep south, meaning he was gone more often, driving further, and having to forge new relationships in an industry built on long-standing contacts. I'm pretty sure they were even making him train his replacement, which must have stung a bit.

These stressors were all happening for my parents right when five additional human beings invaded their home.

We'd moved in on a Friday, and on Monday morning, Blake showed up for what he thought was his first day of paycheck-earning, regularly-houred work. Instead, due to the crossed lines during that one and only phone call, the "meeting" involved the guy telling Blake what special tools to buy for window repair, where to get them, and that he'd let Blake know when business picked up enough to send work his way.

"Try back next week," the owner told Blake.

When Blake later relayed this to me about his "first day of work," I vomited a little in my mouth. "What does that mean?" I asked. "Do you have a job or not?"

"It means 'come back next week,'" Blake replied.

"Well," I said, "a week isn't that long. We have lots to do to get settled in, anyway. It'll be fine. There's no way my mom would let us move down here if he didn't have a job for you. Right?"

Blake shrugged his shoulders, and I wandered off in a daze to stop a sibling battle from evolving into an ER visit.

When Blake went back the next week and heard the same refrain, we knew we were in trouble. It was time for Blake to go look for work, and not come home until he found a job.

He scanned the paper's Help Wanted section. When that didn't show any real options, he went door to door, driving around town, walking into businesses, asking if they had any work. That's how he found a new company that specialized in prefabricated homes. They were built in a factory and dropped off in large pieces at the site. His job would be putting the houses together.

On the spectrum of home carpentry work, you couldn't get much further from the glamorous million-dollar custom homes that he'd been building, and the pay was equally as lacking. He'd have to work a minimum of 70 hours a week to make enough to keep us afloat, not to mention paying for the house in River Falls that we weren't even living in. We had a mantra to calm us whenever the stress seemed unbearable.

"Everything will be golden once the house sells," we told ourselves. "The house will sell. The house will sell. The house WILL sell!"

After the move, I remained a stay-at-home mom. I applied for a few social work jobs and got an offer to work in a women's prison, but we couldn't afford childcare for what they were willing to pay. I found a job at a local coffee shop working part-time nights and weekends, with the idea that Blake and my folks would help with the kids while I was gone. This arrangement was fine for a few months—until our relationships dissolved.

Mom began to resent me almost immediately. The reality of a large, active family in her personal space shattered her dreams of harmonious multigenerational cohabitation, and it soon became a downward spiral that couldn't be stopped. She knew what life was like with small children around, but she was used to them going home at the end of their visit, not sticking around 24/7. Since she wasn't capable of harboring any negative feelings toward her grandchildren, all stress and discomfort from them being underfoot morphed into contempt leveled at me.

For example, baby gates versus knee replacements.

Little Cecilia was a freak of nature. Due to her habit of getting into everything, her habitat had to be restricted to keep her safe and her mother sane. This meant using a series of baby gates to limit her access. So, soon after we moved in, Blake installed a permanent one between the kitchen and main hallway, while I created an obstacle course of temporary baby gates and various pieces of furniture throughout the rest of the house.

I was twenty-nine years old and had been jumping baby gates for years, so I was used to them. My parents were well past the age of hurdling barriers, and the gates wreaked havoc on their joints. Each time they had to stop, reach down, and open the gate before passing through added to their growing well of contempt.

My mother was also somewhat claustrophobic, and as such, loathed closed doors. She couldn't tolerate closing her bedroom door when she went to bed, which was a problem, because Cecilia often woke up screaming in the middle of the night. While I was accustomed to permanent sleep deprivation, my parents were not, and my mom became cranky after these long, loud nights. Understandably, of course.

One day, I suggested that she shut her door.

"It's my house," was something near her response, if not the exact words. "Why should I have to change for you!"

My parents have always been meticulously clean, maintaining an environment two steps below hospital standards. By then, I had shifted into a nice (and sane) "center-range" on the cleanliness spectrum. I deep cleaned monthly, and tidied after meals and playtime, but my parents wanted me to clean the house from top to bottom every other week.

I said I could manage half the house once a week, and the other half the next, but only if I could get help managing the kids while I scrubbed the toilets and polished the 3,000 pieces of antique furniture they owned. Even this arrangement left them perpetually unsatisfied it seemed.

We couldn't come up with a solution for the food quandary, either. Feeding five people on a tight budget is hard, but even harder when sharing refrigerator space and mealtimes with two people who'd earned the privilege of eating steak instead of tuna casserole. We discussed a range of tactics for negotiating the conflicts between our different stages in life. I offered to cook our own meals and keep separate groceries, but that didn't satisfy my mother.

"How am I supposed to say 'no' to the kids when they want the better food we're eating?" she asked. "You're setting me up to be the mean grandma!"

I offered to hand over our monthly food budget, and let them have complete control over the food.

"Then we'd have to do all the shopping while you just lounged around," she said. "No way."

Alternatively, I offered to do the shopping.

She just glared, as if I was a fool to suggest such a thing. When I gave up and wailed, "What do you want me to do?" She walked away.

As the weeks stretched into months, my mother's unhappiness deepened. I tried to empathize with her in an effort to head off what felt like a car accident in slow motion.

"I'm sure that it feels like we have taken your home from you," I said one day. "There are so many of us and we are always here. This is not our house, but it is the only home we have right now."

I thought I'd made a good effort to bridge the widening gap between us, but then, I started getting phone calls from my brother and sister. My mother had been calling them, rather frequently it turned out, to let them know just how awful I was being to her.

"She says that my home is now her house because there are more of them than us!" she'd told them. "She won't clean anything unless someone is watching the kids for her, and then she can only be bothered to do half the job. I basically have to raise those kids for her."

Mom also resented my socializing. I was finally living in the same town as my oldest and dearest friends, but since I was too poor to go out—and, you know, had a bunch of kids to take care of—that when I socialized, I wanted my friends and their kids to come over. It didn't seem like it would be a problem.

Historically, my parents had an open house culture. They housed interns for years, hosted numerous parties, and generally loved company. Throughout my entire life, they had taken in complete strangers, and always preferred having my friends come over rather than I go to theirs. Once we settled back in, and I reverted to my habit of inviting friends over, my mother became livid at me for filling her house with strangers.

"Strangers!" I screamed. "You let Daisy move in when I went to college! You've known Iris for more than a decade, and all of her children since they were born!"

It got uglier when my brother Jack came down for Cecilia's birthday. By that point, my mother's contempt was feeding itself every day. There was nothing I could do to appease her. During the party, my brother took me aside to dress me down for making Mom miserable. I tried to explain the situation.

"Think about it," I pled to Jack. "I've had my own house for years, you've been in all of them. Have I ever been a deplorable housekeeper? I've always taken care of my kids. Do you really believe I'm neglecting them?"

"Shut up," he responded. "You're under their roof, so whatever they say is what goes."

My final effort was to point out that Dad was upset—actually upset—because Blake had mowed the lawn the wrong way. The. Wrong. Way. My dad's claim was, and I'm quoting him here, that "his stride is too long." Seriously?

This was everyday life in that house. We couldn't do anything right.

After watching my mother descend into what I can only describe as a "deep depression," I sat down with her and my father. I looked her in the eyes and spoke as carefully as I could. I still loved them after all and was thankful for their generosity, but it was very clear our living arrangements weren't going to work.

"Mom, you are so miserable having us in this house," I said. "I would rather live in a trailer than watch you suffer any more."

I then asked her to repeat back to me what I just told her.

"You said you'd rather live in trash than spend another moment with me because I am such a miserable person," she said.

I turned to my dad and asked him if that's what I said. He took a deep breath, looked at his feet, shook his head, and whispered, "No, that's not what you said at all."

He slowly met my mother's furious gaze, and she stormed off.

With just the two of us in the room, he let me know in no uncertain terms that no matter what she said or did, he'd back her up. That I should never think he'd ever side with me against her, no matter how irrational she became.

"She's my wife," he said, "and she will always be right." Dad seemed to see the situation for what it was, but he also lived by the motto "happy wife, happy life."

The crux of the situation was that we were living within numerous contradictions. We weren't guests in their home, so they couldn't treat us that way. The house wasn't our house, but it *was* our home, because we were living in it. My mom wanted to be the matriarch, but I wasn't giving up my responsibility of raising my kids and managing my family. We were two separate families at very different stages in our lives, and the boundaries blurred in horrible ways.

Despite this conflict, the girls remained my primary source of joy.

All three had adapted quickly to their new environment. Amara loved her new school, made several friends right away, and spent hours climbing trees in the backyard and tending the garden that she and my dad had planted.

I got Sophie into a preschool program that was part of the local vocational technology school, where the preschoolers were outnumbered two-to-one by the high school girls there to learn to be daycare providers and teachers. Sophie also loved visiting the "enchanted forest," a wood cove with walking paths and little streams near the house.

And Cea? Well, that little pumpkin got introduced to TV.

In the ten months we lived in that house, she watched more television than during the rest of her life put together. I'd turn on a *Yo Gabba Gabba!* or *Jack's Big Music Show* to get something done for thirty minutes, and the next thing I knew, an hour had passed. Those particular shows were all about music and had a bunch of awesome musicians on as guest performers, so maybe that exposure to alternative music helped her evolve into my little music head later in life. If nothing else, it managed to knock me off my "Kill Your Television" pedestal for a while.

All three girls were especially thrilled to see so much of Iris's four kids. Iris and I had always stayed close despite barriers of distance, time, and finances. One time back in Farmington, Iris and her brood had stayed with us for almost three summer weeks, and the kids had created bonds that never broke.

You could argue we didn't give them much of a choice about being friends, seeing as Iris and I were sister soulmates, but that wasn't the case at all. Left to their own devices, they'd come together like puzzle pieces. It helped that their ages lined up like perfect pairs: Robert/Amara, Andrew/Sophie, Corrin/Cecilia, with Elise just old enough to keep them all in line. Those kids dug each other on a sibling level, and it helped that the gods saw fit to equip them all with their mothers' wicked sense of humor and appreciation for adventure.

It also helped that Iris was a stay-at-home mom in an awkward familial housing situation as well—they were living in her father-in-law's basement. Her husband was supposed to be fixing up an uninhabitable house they'd bought a couple years back, so she understood my plight better than anyone. We'd get our progeny together several times a week, and parented each other's children seamlessly enough that people probably assumed we were lesbians. Nothing would or could ever come between us.

Even Blake.

Over the years, Blake had had minimal contact with Iris, but now that we were living in the same town, he was getting to know her. In time, he developed a huge crush on her. I'm not a jealous person by nature, so my first response was honestly, "of course he has a crush on her, she's awesome!"

I compartmentalized it as a harmless and natural response, until one night he blurted out in the middle of sex, "I wish you were Iris right now." *Ouch.*

I stuffed that down, too, covered it up, and carried on. I didn't know it then, but this crush would grow into an obsession.

October came carried in on winds of change. The first major change happened while we were back in Minneapolis for Blake's brother's wedding. It was the first time my parents had their home to themselves since we'd moved in, but rather than resetting calm, tragedy struck.

We were gone less than 24 hours when my dad called to tell me his brother had died. I needed to fly to Michigan immediately, so I left the girls with Blake, which was a problem because Cecilia was still breastfeeding.

At almost eighteen months old, she was perfectly capable of subsisting on real food, but I hadn't started the weaning process yet for a couple of reasons. First, life at the house was stressful enough without adding the ruckus of a baby constantly screaming for boob time. Second, she was my last baby, and I wasn't completely prepared to end that part of our relationship. But with three days of forced separation in front of us, it was now or never, so that poor pumpkin had to go cold turkey while I suffered through the engorgement issues with a heaping side of guilt.

(However, while I was gone for the funeral, Blake caved and gave Cea a pacifier, so she ended up swapping her boob addiction with a nuk addiction. It was a bit disorienting to suddenly have to buy pacifiers in bulk, and always have them on hand at an age when most kids were giving them up, but oh well.)

Shortly after we returned to Springfield from our trip, Blake, along with everyone else in the company, was cordially invited to a party. Their prizes were pink slips. The company went bust, and so did the last vestiges of our relocation plan.

Fuck it, we were out!

Well, Blake was out at least. He called his old company to get his old job back. He packed a bag, said "adieu" to Illinois, and ensconced himself in his father's house until we pulled the River Falls house off the market and reconvened as a family.

Initially, I wanted to try to ride out the rest of the school year for the girls' sake. I'd felt guilty for pulling them out of their old school in March, and didn't want to double down on any damage that had been done by switching them again in the middle of the school year. But a fateful phone call changed that plan.

One afternoon, while my mom was venting her bile in my general direction, the phone rang and Sophie answered it.

"Hello!" she said. The caller was one of my close friends, Daisy.

"Is your mom there?" Daisy asked.

"Yeah, she is, but Grandma is yelling at her right now," Sophie said. "Mom keeps crying, and saying 'I'm sorry, I'm sorry,' but Grandma keeps yelling."

When Daisy told me about this later, my heart broke. I called Blake and told him that he needed to come get us immediately.

I let my parents talk me into staying through Christmas. My brother, sister, and her kids were all planning on being there, and after all the pain I'd caused my mom, the least I could do was not rob her of having all her grandchildren together for the holiday. It was easier to move the kids over the break, anyway, is what I told myself. But ten months of contempt and resentment came to a boil in the middle of dinner.

Blake and I had spent the lead-up packing up for the move, and my folks were a mixed bag of emotions. Our inability to make living in Springfield a success was a bitter pill for all of us to swallow. They were going to miss the girls and were disappointed we were all moving back. On the other hand, they couldn't wait to get their house back. They'd even already taken down all the baby gates.

And so on Christmas Day, while I went out to run errands, I left the kids with Blake, my brother Jack, and my folks. Despite all of those adults to guard over her, Cecilia managed to worm her way into a bathroom, where she was soon found playing with a razor and sticking toothbrushes in the toilet. Jack was frustrated by that event, but it wasn't until that night's dinner when he finally erupted.

Jack had been slaving away in the kitchen for hours to put a five-course gourmet meal on the table, headlined by crown pork roast. Unfortunately, small children don't have the patience to sit through such things, and shortly before the main course was to be served, all of them made their dissatisfaction obnoxiously apparent.

Cecilia escaped from her high chair, and made a beeline for the family room. Jamal, my sister's three-year-old, had already made his break for the toys. Sophie wasn't about to hang around waiting for an adult meal when she could be up to some kiddie antics, so she brazenly walked away. Amara slipped away last, mumbling something about supervising the little ones.

I excused myself for a moment to set them up with a movie. When I came back to begin dishing out the main course, my brother had started dishing out sides.

So there we were, slowly circling the table, plates of food in our hands. As we spooned and forked out the meals to our family, Jack began shooting his tiny, stabbing criticisms in my direction.

"Can't you even try to control your children?" he asked.

"No, I'm sorry," I deflected with humor. "I lost their remote controls."

He wasn't going to let it go. "Don't be a smart ass," he said. "It's not funny."

"Why don't you get back to me about how to raise my kids after you've managed to make a couple of your own."

"I don't need to have kids," he said, "to know how incompetent you are."

It devolved further. The rest of the family just sat back and watched the show. I finally snapped.

"Go fuck yourself!" I shouted, and dropped the huge platter of meat on an empty chair. I stormed off. These would be the last words I exchanged with my brother for three years. The next time we spoke, it would be about the girls' murders.

At that moment, I wanted to take my kids, run, and never look back. I knew the kids deserved to have one last night with their cousins, and so after dinner, when Blake and I left for the night—we'd been staying at a friend's house to make room for the influx of relatives for the holidays—I loved up on my girls, and left them behind in the chaos.

We returned the next morning and loaded up the last of our things to head back north. But because the universe is an evil bitch with a nasty sense of humor, we couldn't just ride off into the sunset. No, that'd be too easy. Instead, we had to fight through the nastiest and most bizarre weather I've ever traveled through. Miles of thick fog, followed by tornado warnings, and when we finally got the fuck out of Illinois, we were welcomed in Wisconsin with a full-blown blizzard.

Blake was driving the moving truck with Amara riding shotgun, while I drove the minivan with Cecilia and Sophie crammed among the house plants. George, a rubber tree plant I'd raised from a small pot to the size of a large man, took up most of the center aisle. My co-pilot was Blake's miter saw, strapped in securely with the seatbelt.

On the last leg of our journey, we'd stopped to grab grub and swap Amara and Sophie. Blake was ready for the trip to be done, so he sped off and soon lost us. Outside of Tomah, about two hours from River Falls, the road turned to a sheet of ice and visibility went to nothing. That's when I went off the road and slammed into a ditch.

By the time I got there, the ditch was a party. Because of the horrible conditions, there were already about a dozen cars down there, padding my arrival. No one was hurt except for poor George, but the van was totaled.

To add to our misery, Blake's cell phone was turned off, so he had no idea what had befallen us until he got home and we didn't show. We waited for almost an hour before a tow truck finally moved us to the Walmart Super Center, the only place in Tomah that was open 24/7.

I spent the hours wandering aimlessly through Walmart, two miserable children in tow, humbled to my core. Never before had I felt like such a complete and utter failure. All my plans had gone up in flames, and when I prayed for rain, the universe offered piss instead. I felt like I'd hit rock bottom. My parents and siblings despised me. My husband lusted after my best friend. Financially, we were starting from scratch, and now we needed to buy a new car.

As I made my 100th circuit of Walmart while we waited for Scott, a family friend, to rescue us, Amara and Cecilia started to giggle. These noises soon became belly laughs bordering on hysteria. I looked around to see what was eliciting such joy from my tired and bored babies, but there was nothing particularly exciting about the housewares section we were walking through. Then, between gasps for air, I heard "Boo!"

Amara had been employing her best peek-a-boo moves to Cea. She was holding up a box of cereal bars in front of her face, deftly maneuvering from behind, shouting "boo!" in a dozen different styles.

Cecilia couldn't get enough of it. When her attention began to wane, Amara made the game bigger. She dodged behind displays and jumped out as I pushed the cart past her hiding spots.

Cea's peals of laughter filled the empty super store and started to fill in the pit of despair that had formed in my soul.

Chapter Nine

Kiss With a Fist

The morning after Blake had me arrested for domestic assault, we sat at the kitchen table talking. Each of us cradled cups of coffee in our hands, and neither had the courage to look each other in the face. I looked out of the window at the playground set in the backyard.

"Do you want a divorce?" I whispered.

At first, I didn't think he heard me, but then he sighed and said, "No."

A beat later, he looked up from the coffee he'd been addressing. "Do you want to leave me?" he asked.

I swallowed down my bitterness and discontent. "Not yet," I said.

This was in September of 2009, nine months after we'd returned to River Falls from the great Illinois debacle.

I had started the year off full of desperate hope born from being settled at rock bottom. I mean, how could we get any lower? We were starting from scratch financially, and had failed to make a go of it in Illinois while seriously damaging my familial relationships. It goes to show that the scales of life can always tip a little further.

Blake was back at the construction company, building houses all over the Twin Cities. We'd cashed in every retirement account we could, and we were able to pay off each debt except the house. We got our bills as

86

low as we could, and began the long climb out of the hole we'd found ourselves in. Babies need to eat, bills need to be paid, and that meant I needed a job.

The timing worked out well. Amara was finishing up second grade with her old crew, and Sophie would be heading into kindergarten in the fall. I'd only have one pumpkin who needed daycare. Going back to work full-time was finally a viable option worth exploring, and so I began the search.

Landing a gig was shockingly easy. Social work, as a profession, is very forgiving about lapses in employment, so the five years I took off to wrangle toddlers didn't hold me back one bit. Quickly, I found a promising job at the Metropolitan Area Agency on Aging as a Health Insurance Counselor and Certified Medicare Specialist and Information Specialist.

I was on their hotline for seniors. My days were spent answering calls from people looking to find services, information about medications and healthcare needs, and comparisons of Medicare plans. Essentially, it was explaining to people in crisis what resources existed that could make their journeys more bearable. It was occasionally challenging, sometimes rewarding, and even a little thrilling—when the phone rang, I had no idea what the call would be about. But it wasn't something I wanted to do very long.

The pay was okay. It covered daycare costs, not much else. But that was fine. We could break even for six months until our costs went down with more kids in school. Anyway, this gave me the experience I needed for a future job, which had its own value.

While finding a job was easy, finding childcare was a nightmare akin to online dating.

On its most basic level, the childcare industry is one that necessitates handing over the most precious parts of one's beating heart to the care and influence of strangers. Was there sincere care, or even possibly love, to be hoped for from their end? Sure! But at the end of the day, it's an exchange of money for services, simple as that. And you never really know if the person described in the ad truly reflects how they are in the flesh.

Also, logistically speaking, I had a lot working against me finding a good fit. I needed a care provider on Amara's bus route: hard. I needed one with three open spots: harder. I needed one that was affordable: virtually impossible.

When we first moved back to town, I had touched base with the family that I'd done daycare for before heading south, and they told me about the lady watching their kids now. Her house wasn't on Amara's route, but the school district provided time for kids to make bus connections possible. She had a great house with plenty of developmentally-appropriate toys and activities for the girls, but the lady was accustomed to catering to school teachers, meaning that the kids had to be picked up an hour before I could hope to leave my desk. She thought she could work a little later than usual, but after the first few days, she decided working past 3:30 p.m. cramped her style too much.

Back to the begging board.

After a few more failures, there I was, my first week back in the workforce with no daycare for my girls. I scrambled, got desperate, ditched most of my expectations, and finally prayed. I was seriously considering options for hiding the kids in my cube when I found Peyton, a licensed home daycare provider who could take all three girls *and* lived on the bus route. Perfect.

Soon, we found out our families had several similarities. Peyton had been a social worker who started a home daycare after her twins were born. And her husband, Dewayne, was a home construction worker, just like Blake. It wasn't surprising, then, that we became close friends.

Working outside the home didn't lessen my home workload. I still did everything I always did, while now also commuting 45 minutes each way to work. And then, within a month of me going back to work, Blake went back to not working.

His company had started "rolling layoffs," a convoluted process of laying off different crews at different times so the guys could tap into unemployment benefits as jobs were spread out. I never fully understood it. Blake's unemployment benefits came through Illinois because of that pink slip party back in 2008, so on the one hand, he had a leg up on his coworkers because he could start collecting more quickly. But on the flip side, he had to deal with an unemployment office in another state with its own set of headaches.

Now, I know what you may be thinking: *Hey, if Blake wasn't working, why wasn't he taking care of the kids?* Here are some excuses.

One: the layoffs were random and unpredictable, so Blake had no idea from day-to-day if he'd be working. Two: Daycares are set up so that you pay for the slot, not the hours of care you're given, meaning that we had to pay for the full month whether we used the time or not. Three, and this is the most important point: even if we could plan around his unemployment, there was no way in hell he'd care for the kids because it would've cut into his game time. Seriously, the notion that Blake could watch the kids was so alien to our lives, we didn't even consider it as a possibility.

It all meant that Blake spent that spring playing video games in an empty house, with random breaks of working. To salt the wound, our neighborhood was filling up with small houses for first time home buyers thanks to the Obama-era Homebuyer Credit. That meant that every time Blake looked outside, he saw building going on without him. So, mostly he just closed the drapes and built up his game characters instead.

At this time in the country, problems had infected the entire housing construction industry. Dewayne, Peyton's husband, was a union guy, but that didn't stop him from having the same work issues Blake had to deal with. But whereas Blake sunk like a stone into his video games, Dewayne had big, delicious dreams of doing something with his life. He wanted to be a chef.

While digging through his options, he figured out that people collecting unemployment can keep their benefits while going to school, as long as they finished their degree within two years. It involved a lot of hoop-jumping and paper-pushing, but it technically could be done. His enthusiasm infected Blake.

Blake had enough credits to get a bachelor's degree within the two years, but only if he buckled down. He decided to go for a degree in Biochem at the University of Wisconsin, River Falls. I agreed to the plan, but with three caveats. One: no more video games, period. Two: no hiding if he was struggling with a class. Three: if he had an English class, I'd write his papers for him. What are partners for, anyway?

As summer came to an end, so did my patience for doing all the work. I was running kids, cleaning house, working, and everything else in between, except mowing the lawn and shoveling snow; I drew the line at outdoor physical-intensive labor. All I wanted from Blake was a steady paycheck and a little attention. That frustration led to what was likely our defining moment of 2009.

One night after the kids were in bed, Blake and I walked across the street to socialize with our neighbors. This meant sitting in their garage and bullshitting while drinking White Russians. Every 20 minutes or so, I'd walk back across the street to check on the kids, and after my third or fourth cocktail, I decided it was time to check in one last time before retiring for the evening. Before I went, I let Blake know that I'd appreciate his company in the wink-bedroom-wink-wink. He said he'd join me in a bit, so I went back, checked on my sleeping beauties, and got ready for romance.

I waited for a full hour before finally blowing out the candles, putting my clothes back on, and storming back across the street. That fourth or fifth drink *may* have kicked in, and any subtlety I *may have* possessed was long gone. The details have been misplaced along with a large portion of my dignity, but it went a little something like this.

I burst into the garage and interrupted Blake and two buddies who were in the middle of some hysterical story.

"You need to come home now!" I shouted. "I've been waiting over an hour for you to show up!"

The guys stopped laughing and all turned to stare at me. The other men crossed themselves to ward off shrewish wife jinxes and thank their lucky stars I wasn't their own personal ball and chain. Blake glared daggers as he set down his drink. He stalked out of the garage with his tail between his legs, and we headed home. I rushed to keep up, verbally vomiting my displeasure the entire way.

Once we were inside, we went to the bedroom. The kids were sleeping and neither of us wanted to risk waking them, so we proceeded to have our vicious fight in measured, whispered voices. I demanded that if he couldn't do anything else around the house, the least he could do was put out once in a while.

He let me know that treating him like an errant dog that needed its leash yanked in front of others wasn't exactly an aphrodisiac.

As things often do in marital disputes, what started as a fight about one thing evolved into a fight about all things. I don't remember who said what, but when he tried to walk away from me, I grabbed his shoulders and told him that he couldn't keep running away.

The next thing I knew, I was smashed between his back and the wall.

He stomped on my feet and pushed against me with all 200 pounds of his muscle. I couldn't move. I was trapped. All I could think to do was bite. So, I bit him through his cotton shirt until he released me.

He finally did, and I fell to the floor and sobbed. I crumpled into a heap on the beige carpet, wishing I could disappear. I turned off the lights, crawled into bed, pulled the covers up over my head, and lay there thinking about my farce of a marriage. And then, I heard Blake talking to someone.

I crept into the stairwell, and that's when I realized he'd called the police.

"What are you doing!" I wailed. "Don't do this! If the police come, we could lose the kids, I could lose my license! This is serious, Blake!"

He ignored me and went to sit on the stairs by the front door to wait.

I stood in the hallway, hugging myself, not wanting to get too close to Blake, not knowing where else to go.

Finally they arrived, and I answered the door. I'd love to say I was cool and collected, but I couldn't stop crying. I was terrified, but still with it enough to talk through our options.

Wisconsin has great domestic violence laws, which means that once a call is made, someone's probably getting arrested. In this situation, if I had pushed that it was mutual or that he crossed a line, we both would have been arrested, and the kids would've been sucked into the system. But Blake was the one with a horrible bite mark on his back—as far as I know, he still has a scar from it—and he had called for help. So, I was going to jail no matter what either of us said at that point.

Once he saw me get cuffed, Blake tried to recant his accusations. He became slightly belligerent and angry when the officers wouldn't cease and desist, and the cops stepped aside to let me talk him down. I told Blake that all that mattered now was that the girls *not be* affected, that we'd deal with the rest later. That got him to stop yelling.

To this day, I believe Blake called the police because he wanted them to yell at me, to confirm that he was a victim of a shrewish wife, to provide him with some card he could pull out whenever I tried to hold him accountable for something.

After I was placed in the back of the police car, I looked out the window and saw Blake standing on the front porch. He looked so confused, like a child who just figured out their actions have consequences. Even now, I can still see him standing there, watching the cruiser pull away from the house, holding the brochures to the local battered women's shelter that the police had given him. He stood vigil until we were out of sight, and then called the neighbors to help him figure out how to rescue me.

I was mugshoted, fingerprinted, and booked into the county jail. As I was led to my cell, I saw a guy in an adjacent cell. He'd stripped naked and was flinging himself against the cell door. Fortunately, the cells had reinforced windows instead of bars, which protected me from any bodily fluids. It was a helpful reminder that as bad as things are, they could always be worse.

While I was stewing in the slammer, Blake had one of the guys from the garage hang-out come over to the house to stay with the girls, who were still asleep, thank god. The guy's wife drove Blake, who was too drunk to drive, to the jail to bail me out. Three or four hours later, we filled out the paperwork and I left the slammer. Needless to say, it was a tense ride home.

The next day was Sunday, and I spent it wallowing in shame. Monday morning came, and I began the work of cleaning up the mess.

I called the county attorney's office to figure out how I could "undo" my arrest. They directed me to a team of victims' advocates. Later, they'd help carry me through the days and months after the girls were murdered. Ironically, my first contact with them was as a perpetrator of domestic violence. They set me up in a program, where I agreed to participate in marriage counseling, to not drink alcohol, and basically not behave like a criminal asshole for six months. In return, I wouldn't be formally charged with a crime and my record would be clean.

Blake went to two marriage counseling sessions before declaring he was, and I'm quoting here, "Not dealing with this shit."

He wasn't up for participating in any process that would require him to change. I was worried his refusal to take part would violate my program agreement, but my therapist was kind enough to write an explanation, and the district attorney's office confirmed that as long as I did the therapy, I was in compliance. I graduated in March of 2010.

I may not have had a criminal record, but I did get a giant public humiliation trophy.

I'd often read the crime reports in my small town paper to be entertained by stories of drunken college students wandering into stranger's homes or tales of lawn ornament desecrations.

After I was arrested, I went online and saw a small blurb summarizing my night from hell and was relieved that no names had been mentioned. But my digital-only habits kept me from knowing that the paper's print copies included a lot more detail, like the names of the alleged offenders, in this case, Jessica Schaffhausen.

When next Sunday came around, I was ambushed at church. Shortly after service, an acquaintance from my women's circle approached me.

"I saw you were arrested for domestic assault," she said. "Are you conducting a social experiment to highlight the discrepancies in support for male victims of spousal abuse?"

"Yup," I responded, without missing a beat. "I decided to risk my job and children to prove that men can be victims, too."

I appreciated her creative thinking, and overall, it helped that people who knew me, even tangentially, couldn't see me as a violent abuser. That Blake was over a foot taller than me and outweighed me by 50 pounds wasn't lost on many, either. But that didn't stop others from looking at me and imagining the violence I must be capable of if such a big guy had to call the cops. It was a humiliating experience to know that people had a distorted peek into a very painful event in my life. I mean, what kind of mother gets drunk and bites her husband hard enough for the cops to drag her off to jail?

Life goes on. September rolled forward, and I sent Amara off to third grade, Sophie to kindergarten, and Blake to his junior year of college, take two.

Amara was pumped to be back doing her thing. She came home overflowing with details about how great her classroom was, and how she couldn't wait for her first test.

When Sophie got back from her first day of kindergarten, the only detail she was willing to divulge was that she would get to have a whole class just about art. How fantastic was that!

Blake's first accomplishment, meanwhile, was to thoroughly fuck up his unemployment and land us on welfare for six months.

Apparently, he didn't get all the paperwork done, and as a result, we had no income from him for six months. I made $35,000 that year, which for a family of five, was simply not enough. So, I got us some food stamps, acquainted myself with the food shelf, and figured out supplemental medical assistance. It was a sign of the times that my professional job required a license but didn't pay me enough to avoid the programs I used to help others during the day.

Amara, god bless her, took it upon herself to sign up for a special school program to battle childhood hunger. Every Friday, a child could pick up backpacks filled with donated food, and so that's what Amara did. I know other kids noticed, but Amara never complained. She was just happy to contribute. This is why after her death, I chose the River Falls Community Food Pantry as the charity to donate to in her memory.

Eventually, Blake's paperwork got straightened out, and we got back payments for the unemployment. Blake was doing well in college, and life eased up for a while. Soon, 2009 turned into 2010, and the emotional rollercoaster slowed a bit. We enjoyed the humdrum between the peaks and valleys, the deepest one yet to come.

A big part of my therapy during that time was realizing I couldn't control anyone except myself. Especially not my partner. A combination of this lesson, along with spending my workdays witnessing the plights of those with really awful chronic health conditions, led me to find my new religion: health and exercise!

For my thirty-first birthday, I bought a scale and committed to a new way of living. I lost 25 pounds in six months, then decided to get fit. I welcomed legendary trainer Tony Horton into my life. I would spend an hour and a half every day working out. I still recall Horton's mantras that were drilled into my brain. I sincerely owe my survival to the years of training I had with him, before, during, and after losing my girls.

The summer found me in a new position with a much higher salary. To celebrate, Blake put us ten grand in debt by buying electronics and furniture.

We needed the furniture—we were still using a moving box with a tablecloth as our bedside table next to our frameless mattress—but we didn't need a brand-new living room set. We needed a television, but we didn't need a Bose Surround Sound System to go with a giant flat screen. In retaliation, I perpetrated my first act of blatant marital defiance: I got a kitten.

Blake was always anti-pet. He grew up in a house that was cat- and dog-free due to his mother's allergies. While him and his siblings were allowed to have rats, giant cockroaches, or birds, nothing they had would reach the level of a family member.

When we were in our first home, my parents dropped off the two cats I had in high school. They were middle-aged men at that point and greatly resented being kicked out of their home and forced into a new-to-them family. Amara's toddler style affection was met with skin puncturing bites and scratches. Then, they started having very expensive kidney issues I simply could not afford to treat. The only option I had was to surrender them to the humane society, who promised me they could be kept together. I left them at the shelter, while guilt stayed with me.

That fall found me ready to rebel. I was pissed off, and tired of the roles we were playing, of Blake doing whatever he wanted with no consideration for anyone else, and me always having to be the team player. It seemed like such a silly, small thing getting a kitten, but it was important. I didn't consult him, just brought home Opal, a black and grey striped cat with lovely patches of orange. Amara, Sophie, and Cea loved her instantly.

We welcomed other souls into the house that year, too. First to move into our unfinished basement was Megan, Blake's step-sister and Cecilia's godmother, and one of my best friends. She came to live with us for a few months while she transitioned from living with her mom and her intolerant stepfather, into her complete independence. Megan and Amara got along fine, and Megan and Cea always had the special bond of godparent/godchild, but the true dynamic duo was Sophie and Megan. Megan could roll with Sophie's sass and appreciate her jagged edges without getting cut.

One of my favorite memories is them at the kitchen table. In the middle of a conversation, Megan turned to Sophie and said, "Sophie, you're the love of my life!"

"Megan," Sophie responded, "you're the stupid of my life."

Megan couldn't stop laughing long enough to call her a little shit, even though she really wanted to.

Megan's girlfriends during those months also enjoyed spending time with our family. Kay regaled Amara with tales of being discriminated against during her time in the Armed Services. And Farrah, the one Megan eventually left us to move in with, taught Sophie to beatbox. I really think that some of Amara's activism nature was rooted in her exposure to these fantastic and strong women who suffered because of who they loved.

After three months, Megan moved out. Three months later, our next stray moved in: Elliot, Blake's seventeen-year-old cousin.

Elliot's family was very devout Catholics, and struggled immensely when Elliot came out of the closet during his senior year of high school. I know from my own years in social work what can befall a young man who's suddenly homeless, so Elliot stayed with us for a few months until the emotions between him and his parents settled down. Elliot and his friends and boyfriend were all fantastic with the girls. It was a nice novelty to suddenly have so much more testosterone in the house, and gave my girls the opportunity to see that love can exist between all types of people.

That was a transformative year for me as a mother, too. I went from being punk rock mom to soccer mom and troop leader. It wasn't my choice. I was tricked.

Dawn, Amara's BFF's mom, begged me to sign Amara up for traveling soccer because they were desperate to fill the team. Dawn offered to help me out by getting Amara to and from games and practices, and Amara was excited to give it a shot. The next thing I knew, my weekends and evenings were spent shouting random words while trying to learn the lingo. I never did master the subtleties of offside kicks, throws, or whatever else it is they do. But what I lacked in understanding, I made up for in enthusiasm, and more importantly, snacks.

Once we settled back into River Falls, I signed both girls up to be in a troop. Amara went in at a higher level, while Sophie started off in the kindergarten group. Amara's troop was run like a machine by one of the other moms, so all I had to do was drop her off and pick her up.

Sophie's troop needed more of my time and effort, and the troop leader slyly inquired if I'd be willing to help her out once in a while. I knew enough to dodge cookie mom duty, but the next thing I knew, I was in a library meeting room sitting in a circle, chanting over candlelight, and taking some kind of vow. I shit you not. Troops are not to be fucked with.

Anyway, both girls loved it, so I did my duty. Amara eventually chose soccer over the troop when the schedules began to conflict, but Sophie stayed in until her dying day.

Meanwhile, Cecilia loved daycare. Hell, she just loved life. She was happy to run amok and be a kid. Peyton's twin daughters were almost the same age as Cea, and they all ran around like a pack. They'd have sleepovers and tea parties, and spend all day playing. Cea fit in seamlessly everywhere she went.

Sophie, on the other hand, was spiky edges covered in venom. She was adept at finding people's weaknesses and trying to toughen them up. For instance, I constantly found myself telling Sophie to stop making Peyton, a very tender-hearted woman with a lot of insecurities, cry. But whenever I did, Sophie just grinned her wicked little grin.

"Peyton cries too easy," she explained.

Another day, she was waiting for the bus in front of Peyton's home with a girl from next door. The girl's father was watching from inside when he noticed an older man stop to take a picture of the girls. He ran out onto the porch, but the man had already moved on.

The next thing I know, police were called in to interview my baby girl. After plenty of drama and speculation, I took Sophie aside to ask her what had happened.

"I was waiting for the bus and this guy was walking around taking pictures," she told me. "So I hollered at him. 'Hey mister, what are you doing?' He says he's taking pictures of the beautiful trees and leaves. So, I tell him that I'm beautiful, that he should take my picture, too."

In about two minutes, my confident and sassy first grader heckled a man into taking her picture and started a pedophile witch hunt. We survived the rest of the fall without any more police encounters for any of us.

The year wrapped up and I was feeling hopeful. Blake was doing well in school. The kids were happy and healthy. I had a job I was succeeding at. I felt like things were finally under control. My marriage wasn't stellar, but it never had been. My answer to the "do you want a divorce question?" was still "No, not yet."

But a lot can change in twelve months' time. College can be ditched, depression can descend, and fidelity can be destroyed. In a year, Blake and I would file for divorce.

Chapter Ten

Black Cadillacs

The early afternoon sun streamed in through the living room window and reflected off Amara's glasses as she sat on the couch, comfortably lost in one of *The Sisters Grimm* books. Sophie came skipping in from outside and began to leap and dance around the room.

"I love Simon!" Sophie announced with glee, practically singing. "I loooooove Simon! I am going to marry Simon!"

Amara sighed. She gently closed her book and looked at Sophie with the disdain of an old crone.

"Sophie," Amara started, "one of these days Simon is going to disappoint you."

Sophie was undeterred by the warning. She stuck her tongue out, blew a raspberry at her sister, and ran back outside to see what Simon and the other neighborhood kids were up to. But as usual, Amara was proven right.

Within hours, Sophie decided Simon was no longer worthy of her affections, that he was, in fact, a selfish jerk. The deal-breaker: he wouldn't share his new remote-controlled car.

In 2011, the girls moved further down their path of independence and growth, and we all figured out how to detect the selfish jerks in our lives.

Cecilia, now almost three, was ready for her next level of education, but Peyton, her daycare provider at the time, was only able to provide basic childcare, not a preschool curriculum. Luckily, I was able to get Cecilia into the UWRF CHILD Center, a phenomenal institution with a fantastic staff. As an added bonus that was, and is, exceedingly rare in the childcare world, Cecilia had not just one, but *two*, men working in her classroom! This was huge for me, because I wanted her to know that men could be caregivers, too.

Cea blossomed in this new environment, instantly making what felt like to me a thousand new friends. She also discovered her true love: glue. She'd use about a gallon a day to create three-dimensional masterpieces, often accentuated with organic materials. One of her last creations began with a piece of blue construction paper, a vast puddle of glue, and a pile of sticks, leaves, grass, with one large twig standing straight up. It was adorned with half an eggshell that had been dusted with glitter. Her relationship with the sticky stuff was so legendary that, after she died, the daycare staff and friends left bottles and sticks of glue on her headstone.

While Cea was working on her art, Amara and Sophie were too old for the daycare center, so I decided it was time for them to embrace the life of latchkey kids.

They were seven and ten at the time, and had demonstrated themselves to be more than capable of getting themselves on the bus in the morning and home safe after school. Every state has different rules for when children can be left unsupervised, so I did some research. I found that Wisconsin didn't have a set age, just guidelines for assessing a child's readiness for limited independence. I then called child protection to doubly cover my ass, and they confirmed.

After all of that ass-covering, I sat my girls down to have a little chat. They were predictably pumped to embrace this new milestone, so I tested them by peppering them with scenarios.

"Someone rings the doorbell?" I started.

"Pretend we aren't home," they both answered quickly, like game show contestants at the same time. I upped the ante.

"One of you falls and gets hurt?" I asked.

"Call 9-1-1 if it's really bad," Sophie chimed in.

"But call you, if we can walk it off," Amara said simultaneously.

"Aliens land in the backyard."

"Do not engage," they said, not missing a beat. "Retreat to a secure position and observe until we can determine their intentions," Amara added.

"And?" I prodded.

"Oh, and do *not* call 9-1-1," they both said. "It could start an intergalactic war," Sophie responded.

They couldn't have been better prepared.

Our new routine wasn't that different from our old one. We'd wake up around the same time, grumpiness randomly assigned overnight to give each day some variety. I'd make myself presentable while Cecilia tried on and dismissed no fewer than three outfits before finally settling. Cea and I would bid adieu to the older girls, hop in the car, and rock out to whatever 89.3 FM "The Current," our favorite public radio station, was jamming.

Cea was my budding music head, and the ride to daycare often involved dissections of each song. Sometimes, she liked the beat but not the singing, other times vice versa; when "Gangster" by tUnE-yArDs came on, she declared that the song had it all. And then I'd drop her off at daycare, where I was lucky to get a hug and kiss before getting dumped for all of her friends.

Back at home, Sophie and Amara would bicker while eating breakfast and gathering school supplies. Sophie would then begin testing limits, mostly Amara's, especially as they waited to get picked up by the bus.

For a little while, she'd taunt her uber-responsible eldest sister by acting like she wasn't getting on the bus. Amara would try to make her, but this only resulted in Sophie cackling like a witch and running amok, proving how uncontrollable she was. After one morning, that match of wills resulted in the girls missing the bus, so I sat them down to have another chat.

"Whose behavior can you control?" I inquired of my little heathens.

Amara scrunched up her face in serious thought.

"If I can't control Sophie, what makes you think you can?" I pushed.

"But Mom, what if she misses the bus or runs off?" Amara pled.

I could see Amara was frustrated. She liked things that were logical and followed a formula, which her sister was the antithesis of.

"Then she will deal with the consequences of her actions, not you," I told her. "You are not in charge of her, you are only in charge of yourself."

I turned to Sophie, who was biding her time. She knew she had to deal with the lecture, and she also knew that my point was to take away her power to torture Amara, not actually make her change.

"Sophie," I calmly said, "do you understand that no matter what you do, the only one getting in trouble is you?"

She shrugged. "I understand, Momma."

Once I made it clear that Amara was not her sister's keeper, and that only Sophie would be held accountable for Sophie's actions, the conflicts seemed to end.

That was the extent of my troubles with the girls that year. Overall, it was great having the girls at home after school. During this time, Amara had fallen in love with cooking and baking. The science and math it required thrilled her nerdy soul, and the results fed us all. The first dish she mastered was to be her favorite, tuna noodle casserole. Soon, she moved onto more complex baking, and by the time she died, she was making pies from scratch and concocting a perfect meringue. Not an easy feat.

All three girls stepped up and pitched in according to their abilities. Even the littlest did her own dishes, unlike their father.

The year had begun with the hope of potential. Blake had aced Organic Chemistry, reportedly the hardest class that his degree required, meaning the light at the end of the educational tunnel was getting brighter and closer. But to Blake, rather than signaling opportunity and freedom, the light looked like a train of responsibility barreling down upon him.

I don't know exactly when things started to fall apart. It felt like one moment he was excelling in his classes, active in the Chemistry Club, and even working in the lab after school. And then the next, he was a drop-out again.

In late February of 2011, I had hemorrhoid surgery, just another fantastic part of having a body that's pushed out a bunch of babies. So, I was home for a few days of recovery, and for the first time in our marriage, Blake offered to tend to me.

"I can talk to my professors and miss a couple of classes to be around after you have your surgery," he said.

"Really?" I was shocked. "That'd be nice, if it doesn't mess up your school stuff."

The pain drugs dulled my natural skepticism, so at first, I didn't question this unusual offer. Of course, tending to me was mostly double-speak for being around the house when he was supposed to be at class. But, hey, beggars can't be choosers, right?

One night around two a.m., nature called and I hobbled into the bathroom to deal with what I feared would be worse than childbirth. *That* area of my body radiated pain, and the idea of having to use it in the cut-up, bleeding state it was in terrified me. I began with some deep calming breaths, then sat on the toilet to begin the process. The pain from simply farting and slightly bearing down was so obliteratingly awful, I passed out, and hit my head on the bathtub.

Hours later I came to, shivering on the bathroom tile. My doctor diagnosed me with a concussion, ordered me not to drive anywhere for a few days, and to chug a bottle of laxative before trying to go to the bathroom again.

So, yes, technically I gave myself a concussion trying to shit.

This extension of my recovery time forced Blake to confess something to me. He waited for the kids to be in bed, and then for my night-time pain meds to kick in, before sitting across from the couch where I had laid down. He said he had something to tell me.

"That I'm a goddess of beauty despite recent horrifying events in the bathroom?" I dryly tried to guess.

Blake didn't laugh.

That was troubling. He always got my jokes. We had an unspoken agreement that, no matter what, he'd always find me to be hilarious and witty. This breach in our contract raised alarm bells.

"I stopped going to my classes a couple of weeks ago," he told a spot about five feet from my face.

What followed was me cussing enough to make a construction worker blanche, wailing like a banshee, and breathing deeply while wiping tears from my eyes and snot from my face. Finally, after that exorcism, I was ready to deal with our family's latest curveball.

"Why?" I asked, finally calm again. "You're so close to graduating."

He explained about no longer being able to get a passing grade in one class, that he had passed the point of no return. I recalled when I'd gone to college, how every report card was a surprise because I'd lacked the math skills, or desire, to calculate my grades. But not Blake, who recorded every assignment, every pop quiz, every project to accurately calculate his GPA every day. So, when he gave me some convoluted explanation about a physics grade being beyond recovery, I almost believed him.

Almost.

"Bullshit!" I yelled. "You aren't even halfway through the semester, how can it be impossible to turn it around?"

"Fine!" he admitted. "The truth is, I have to do a presentation in front of over a hundred people for my senior project, and the thought of standing on a stage and being judged makes me want to puke. I can't do it." Then he shouted. "I will *not* do it!"

I started making suggestions, but he shut down. Ever try to convince a brick wall to move? That's what talking to him was like once he made up his mind. And then, after all that, for the first time in my marriage, I saw him cry.

"Don't leave me," he whispered.

I pictured the domino effect this would have on our finances, our future, and our girls.

"I just paid your tuition for the semester," I said. "Can we get any of it back?"

It turned out that, no, we could not. If he'd dropped out two weeks sooner, we'd have been in the clear, but instead, we'd essentially just donated about $3,000 to the university.

"Start looking for a damn job tomorrow!" I said, which was going to be my last word on the subject. Then, I remembered spring break.

The girls and I had a tradition of spending spring break in Springfield, Illinois. Glamorous, I know, but we couldn't afford anything tropical. Plus, I'd have to take the week off work to stay with the girls anyway, so it was the "Patch" with friends and family, or nothing. This year, we had plans to stay with Iris and her kids, since my parents were spending their tax season vacation with my sister in South Dakota.

"If you think I'm going to leave you here by yourself to play video games for a week while we go to Springfield, you've got another thing coming!" I said. Then demanded, "You will come with us and help, and I mean *really* help, with the kids."

I went to bed in a huff that night, and we left for Iris's a few weeks later. By that time, she'd left her husband, and was renting a large house with plenty of space to accommodate our brood. It helped that the kids tended to just sleep in a pile like a bunch of puppies.

Iris was, and still is, a superwoman. At that time, she was raising four kids, working three jobs, and even taking some college classes. Even without all of those balls to juggle, it's damn hard to keep a clean house, and the goddess bless her, even she will admit that she tends to be messy. It was set to be a great trip, except for one vital thing: I'd forgotten about Blake's crush on Iris.

"Forgotten" is maybe the wrong word. I had buried it, ignored it, simply tried to deny its existence. It was there, no doubt, and you can imagine how I felt when, after a trip to the park with a gaggle of kids, Iris and I walked in to find Blake on his hands and knees scrubbing her kitchen floor. As far as my heart was concerned, cleaning her house was the equivalent of buying her a diamond necklace.

"Are you cleaning her kitchen?" I said, aghast.

"I'm just trying to help out," he said from the floor.

"Well, there is a first for everything," Iris responded.

I'm still not sure if she was referring to Blake being helpful, or it being the first time the floor had been mopped. But his attempts at seduction didn't stop there.

During this trip, Iris had given her bedroom to Blake and I, while she crashed on one of the kids' beds. One night, Blake left me sleeping soundly while he crept downstairs to blast music.

Iris woke up, and when she did, she found him standing in her doorway. She was disoriented and thought maybe he couldn't figure out how to turn off the music, so she stumbled downstairs and turned it off. She later told me that he'd followed her, and once the music was silenced, he whispered to her.

"See, no one can hear anything," he whispered. "We could do anything, and no one would know."

Iris was half-asleep and confused. She shook her head, told him "No," and went back to bed, shutting the door firmly behind her. She managed to shut him down that night, but she'd soon learn the persistence that Blake was capable of.

I, of course, didn't know anything about this at the time, and so, to me, the rest of the week was nothing but fun and games. The kids were rollicking around, while Iris and I stayed up too late, laughed too loud, and wallowed in each other's company. I didn't notice her avoiding Blake or notice him skulking after her. My focus was on his lack of employability, not his lack of desirability.

After a week, we returned home. The girls and I fell back into our routines, but Blake fell into a deep, catatonic depression. He performed the bare minimum needed to get his unemployment, which meant applying for jobs, and demonstrating an inclination to earn a paycheck again. Around the house, he stopped doing the few chores he had, like taking out the garbage or mowing the lawn. One day, I came home early from work to find him sitting on our bed, staring at the wall.

"Have you been here all day?" I asked.

No response.

"Seriously, have you moved at all?"

He turned his head slightly in my direction.

"Alright, enough is enough," I said. "You're going to see a therapist, or a doctor, or a something!"

He sharply turned back to the wall, so I walked around the bed to stare into his eyes.

"Get up, get moving. We are done doing this shit," I said.

This zombie act was grating on my nerves. I grabbed a glass of lukewarm water from the bedside table and threw it in his face. He just stared ahead, not even moving to dry himself. I left him on the bed, dripping water and depression all over the mattress.

The next day, he went to see a doctor, and got a prescription for an antidepressant. That first one had no effect that we could tell, so after a couple of weeks, he got a different one. That caused a 180-degree change in a matter of days. I barely recognized this Blake, suddenly there, participating in life, functioning like a human being. He quickly found a job with a cabinet maker that paid little enough that he still collected unemployment while working forty hours a week. Blake was optimistic about this shift.

"I get to learn fine carpentry work and branch out a little," he said, beaming. "This will help me be more employable, and at least I'm working."

Blake began spending more time with the kids and acting like a normal person, a miracle as far as I was concerned. My fear of Catatonic Blake fed my reverence for these magic pills and dampened any concerns I had about the side effects. Suddenly, he could drink his weight in alcohol and not have any signs of being intoxicated.

He also started behaving in ways I didn't appreciate. One late night, after the kids were in bed and we were hanging in the living room listening to music, he asked what I thought about the idea of an open marriage. I thought he was joking.

"Seriously, Jess!" he said. "You deserve someone who'll take you dancing and out on dates. Why don't you find a boyfriend to treat you right?"

"Why don't you just do all those things for me?" I responded. "I am not interested in finding a boyfriend, just a partner who loves me."

"Think about it," he said.

"Think about it!" I screamed. "Blake, it is nuts. We have kids and a family. I'm not interested in any guy that would be into that kind of set-up. You just want an open marriage so you can go sleep with other women, but still have me at home taking care of you. Fuck that. If you want out of this marriage, get out, but I'm not playing that game."

I assumed it was just a fleeting fantasy, but he kept bringing it up about once a month. I kept responding the same way. Until the day I decided to try to call his bluff.

The summer of 2011 was the summer of Grandma and Grandpa Stout camp and the MN State Shut Down. Amara, Sophie, and Cea spent most of the summer in Springfield going to vacation bible school, art camps, or simply being spoiled by my folks. Three months was a long time to go without seeing my babies. I had planned for sporadic trips down to see them for my own sanity. My job at the time was state-funded, and as a result I was granted a bonus trip right in the middle of the summer. Nothing sweeter than a long vacation on the government's tab. Blake stayed behind to keep working. I had been in Springfield hanging out with the girls for three glorious work-less weeks. Alas the state settled their differences, and I was about to head back to reality. My last night in town, I loved up on my girls, bid them a sweet adieu, and headed over to Iris's house. We got all dolled up, met up with some other lady friends, and hit the town. We had spent our 20s having babies and chasing toddlers, so it was an understatement to say that we had to let off a little steam, and it got kinda wild. There was dancing, drinking, and eventually some flirting. I was shocked to discover that not only was I attractive to young gorgeous men, but that I very much craved their attention as well.

There was one particularly sweet young man. He told me he was an organic farmer, which as far as I knew could have been code for pot-grower, but I still prefer to think of him as lovingly protecting beets from pesticides.

Anyway, one thing led to another, and I found myself back in Iris's kitchen, passionately kissing a man other than my husband. And then another thing led to another, and I found myself in a bedroom with him, trying to remember how the bits and pieces fit together. Then, I began to panic.

Turns out, whispering things like "I get pregnant really easily. Are you sure that condom isn't expired?" and, "Seriously, so easily, like just thinking about getting pregnant and it happens" can be a bit of a turn-off. Let's just say that my experiment in adultery was unsatisfying for all involved.

The next morning, I dropped him off at his car, and barely stopped before kicking him to the curb. My last words to him were "Well, here we go then. Nice meeting you. Very sorry for involving you in my midlife crisis!" as I sped off north.

I spent the entire eight hours driving back weeping copiously and indulging in self-loathing. I felt horribly disgusted with myself. I told Blake about what had happened immediately. I was hoping he'd be jealous and would realize he did not, in fact, want his wife sleeping with other men. Instead, he wanted details.

I was soaking in the bathtub after my long drive and he came in to talk to me about it.

"You have nothing to feel bad about!" he tried to reassure me.

"This is not who I want to be! This is not the marriage I want!" I said.

He started implying that maybe the problem was the guy, that it would be better if I tried again.

"No. You are not listening to me," I said. "I am not doing this again. If I do sleep with another man, it will be because we are through."

I hoped that was the end of it, but nope, he tried to bring it up again the next month. That time I just got up and walked away.

Things were almost at the end with us by then. The dissolution of our marriage wasn't a straight drive from coupled to uncoupled, more like getting stuck in a roundabout.

Back in the spring before school was getting out, the medication had dragged him out of the deepest pit he'd been in, but it wasn't enough to bring him up to the level that the girls and I existed at. He'd mow the lawn, but wouldn't go to soccer games. He'd go to work, but then disappear into a vapid video game for hours.

One night I had to work late, and when I got home, I found my babies hanging out in the living room watching *Howl's Moving Castle*.

"Hey girls!" I chirped as I walked in. "What did you have for dinner?"

"We actually haven't really eaten yet," Amara informed me with one eyebrow cocked. "Dad won't get off the computer. He told us he'd eat with us, but that was almost two hours ago."

I knew there was no point even trying to address it with him, so I whipped up a quick dinner and let my anger simmer.

Weeks later, stressed for time and burdened with bags of groceries, I walked to the computer room and snarled. "Get downstairs and help unload groceries now!" I yelled as Blake was hours into Battle Tetris on Facebook.

My outburst disrupted his clicking and he lost a life. His anger was palatable. He stormed down the stairs into the kitchen, drove his hands into one of the bags of groceries, pulled out a couple of containers of yogurt and flung them around the kitchen.

"There! Happy? I unloaded groceries!" he yelled and stalked back to his game.

A few years back, as a gift from my folks, we'd gotten one of those Willow Tree statues of a couple embracing and set it on the kitchen counter. After he stormed off, my eyes locked onto it. I felt like it was mocking me now as I stood in my kitchen, all covered in yogurt. I felt loneliness in knowing I never really had a partner. I walked over to the statue and knocked it down with the flick of my wrist. It broke on the hardwood floor.

The girls had been watching the whole scene from the living room and walked in.

"We can help clean up, Mommy," Amara softly said.

"No, no, babies," I said, my voice cracking. "I am sorry you saw that. I got it covered. Why don't you go play?"

Sophie picked up the broken statue. "Mom, you broke love!" she said.

"It's okay, honey," I said. "It's just a statue."

"No, it's not," she responded. "It's you and Dad."

Well, that broke me straight down the middle, and the tears that I'd been restraining ran down. I started to see Blake as an anchor, dragging me and the girls down. I remember distinctly deciding that I couldn't leave him when he was seriously depressed. Abandoning him when he was unemployed and barely functioning felt wrong. I didn't hate him, but I couldn't take my kids any further on this downward spiral.

Another loop was thrown at me when we made one of our planned visits down to see the girls and break up the long summer away from them. We spent a couple days at Iris's as a family before we headed north. First, we celebrated her son Andrew's 8th birthday with cake, hula-hooping contests, and cascarones. That was always the best part of our families getting together—instant party every time!

Then, the plan was for Iris and I to go out for a girls' night on the town. At that time, Iris had a fairly serious boyfriend named Tony, so him and Blake watched the kids as we danced and drank and danced some more, before cabbing back home in the wee hours.

When we got back, I said a slurry "goodnight" to all, went upstairs, and crashed. Meanwhile, Iris vomited a few times and didn't make it past the living room couch. Tony stayed with her as she recuperated.

But instead of coming up, Blake stayed downstairs. He paced around the couches, occasionally sitting down, and then smoked on the front porch, hovering like a jealous vulture until Tony spoke up.

"Dude, shouldn't you be upstairs with your wife?" Tony asked him, Iris still passed out next to him.

"You need to leave," Blake said. "Iris doesn't want you here. She told Jess that she's breaking it off with you."

"There is no way I'm leaving her alone with you," Tony told him. "She is drunk, and I'm gonna stay right here and make sure she's safe."

Blake refused to budge until Tony went into the kitchen, retrieved a large knife, and went back to the couch next to Iris. Blake spent the rest of the night sitting in a chair in the next room over. I heard all about it from Tony the next morning.

After that debacle, Blake's crush on Iris was no longer ignorable. I waited until we were back home to confront him.

"What the fuck, Blake?" I said. "Do you not get how weird and creepy that was?"

"You told me she wanted to break up with him," he said.

"Iris's relationship status has absolutely nothing to do with you!" I screamed. "Why would it matter to you who she's dating?"

"If she doesn't want to be with Tony, he shouldn't be hanging around the house."

"What does any of that have to do with *you*? Why weren't you in bed with me?"

"I couldn't sleep with that guy down there all over her," he explained.

On and on it went. I told him that he was pushing for an open marriage because he hoped he could pursue something with Iris. He seemed to absorb that, and then told me he'd drop it. We carried on, circling the drain.

While I was looking for a marital exit Blake was looking for work to cover the bills once his unemployment dried up. He reconnected with his old boss at the construction company, and they told him about their plans to cash in on the oil boom in North Dakota. They offered him a job out there, and the company would pay for room and board, plus a nice salary. The only catch was that he'd live in North Dakota for months at a time.

To me, that was a bonus. I saw this as an out. We could separate without completely disintegrating just yet. I had a theory that life without Blake would be far easier than life with him, but wasn't completely confident in that idea yet. I just needed to test it.

"Absolutely, take it!" I yelled when he told me about the offer.

Blake didn't have a lot of other options, so he took it. He wouldn't ship out until October, and so he continued to work around Wisconsin and Minnesota in the meantime. That meant he was living in a hotel during the week, home on the weekends.

All the while, I'd been seeing the same marriage therapist that I saw after the domestic assault incident to help me work through my growing desire to get out of my marriage. I was stuck in a kind of a purgatory. Should I stay or should I go? As it turned out, I had a breaking point.

During my last weekend of freedom before returning to Springfield to bring the girls home, I invited my good friend Dawn over for wine and girl talk. Usually, whenever I had friends over, Blake would make himself scarce. But this time, he did something different. Blake walked into the living room, said "hello," and subtly filled our wine glasses. He wandered away for a while, came back, poured another round. We weren't paying the least bit of attention. The next thing I knew, I was drunk.

D-R-U-N-K.

Through the haze from my perch in the big comfy chair, I looked over and noticed Blake sitting next to Dawn on the couch. It took a bit for my sloshed brain to process what I was seeing, and then it hit me. Blake was brushing Dawn's beautiful, long hair.

My husband. Sitting there. Brushing her hair.

That's the last thing I remember before Blake shook me awake.

"Dawn left," he said frantically. "I'm worried she was too drunk to drive."

"What?" I slurred.

"I tried to kiss Dawn, and she got upset and left," he confessed.

"I can't think about this now," I said, and sank back into sweet oblivion.

The next day I tried to call Dawn, but she was understandably avoiding me. I was terrified that Blake had just destroyed not only one of my friendships, but one of Amara's closest friendships as well. That was it. I was done.

I talked it through with my nearest and dearest friend Iris, ran it past my therapist, and screamed it from the top of my lungs while weeping in the shower. Finally one day, while he was away for a job somewhere in the middle of Wisconsin, I called him and told him we were through.

"And you know what happens when I put something on my to-do list?" I said.

"You get it done," he replied.

"Well, 'get a divorce' just got put on my to-do list," I told him.

I hung up the phone.

Chapter Eleven

Kiss Me Again

Above me was a steel gray sky as hard as my resolve. Below was a blanket of fallen leaves in jewel tones of reds and yellows. The leaves made a satisfying crunch as I walked over them. I was on the phone with Blake. Again. For a decade, the man would dodge my phone calls, but now here he was calling me twenty times a day.

"Did you think I wouldn't leave you? That I wouldn't follow through?" I asked sincerely. "Did you think I would just keep taking your shit forever?"

"No," he answered. "I just didn't think I'd miss you. And now I miss you, so you should come back."

"Too little too late. I'm done, I'm not coming back," I said and hung up the phone, then put it on silent to ignore his next fifteen calls.

Despite the drastic uptick in phone calls, the divorce process had been incredibly easy so far. We forewent the expense of lawyers and just DIY'd the whole thing. We weren't going to be one of those couples battling over every petty piece of shared history, warring for all the rights they can hold onto. At the time, I was so proud of us! Sure, maybe we couldn't make a partnership work, but we excelled at dissolution. Now, of course, I look back and see that there wasn't a fight because he knew the game was rigged. He was holding a live grenade while I was playing with a cap gun.

After the late August 2011 phone call where I declared the end, things moved at a steady clip. We agreed to wait until the girls were back from their summer with Grandma Louise and Grandpa Rhett to tell them. We decided to follow through with the annual Schaffhausen family camping trip with his father, brothers and their families, and then make our announcement.

Every year since the girls were little, Blake's father, Leo, coordinated an all-family camping weekend. He'd pick a campground with spots available next to each other, and the whole clan would come together for a weekend of hiking, biking, and general togetherness. This was not our first rodeo, and we had receipts from REI to prove it. We bought one of those ginormous tents meant to house a family of five with plenty of space left over for personality conflicts. It should have been fine, despite the marital dissolvement, but it was not our finest hour.

We arrived in separate vehicles, Blake's truck loaded with the camping equipment, my station wagon with the kids and food. We began setting up our temporary compound, but within minutes I heard the foreboding words.

"Ummm, Mom?" came spilling out of Amara's mouth. "I think we have a problem."

I looked over at the tent, then rubbed my eyes, willing it to be a hallucination. Blake stood towering over a saggy green pup tent, built for backyard adventures. The only shelter he'd brought would fit three of us like sardines.

I looked him dead in the eye and said, "If you think you and I are sleeping in the car together, think again." And then stalked off to set up sleeping bags in the back of the station wagon.

The first night, Amara and I snuggled in the car talking about how some people have to live in their cars and how hard that must be. The next night, I was used as a mattress by Sophie and Cea in the tent, virtually smothered under a tangle of limbs. What I'd do to have one more sleepless night with them now.

Solid, sparkling memories were rattled against the bits of fool's gold we tossed in the pan to make it all look shiner than it was. There was a family bike ride that went on for miles. Luxurious blue skies, white wispy clouds, and the sound of rushing water followed us down the path. Amara spotted a bald eagle perched in a tree above, and we all stopped to watch it utterly dismiss us. I reminded her of the eagles that used to land in our backyard.

The girls loved poking at the fire and taunting each other.

"Amara took the fire away from me!" tattled Cea.

"She's too little to be playing with it!" countered Amara.

"You are not Prometheus! Fire is not yours to give or take. It is plenty big enough for you all to poke at it!" I said.

There were aunts, uncles, and cousins to keep the kids from noticing how seldom Blake and I actually spoke to each other. We muddled through the rest of the weekend, always keeping a buffer of kids or duties between us. I'm sure others noticed, but simply chalked it up to the typical ebbs and flows of marriage.

As I was pulling away after the long weekend, the girls all loaded up, I looked in my rearview mirror and saw Blake and his dad leaning on the tailgate of his truck. Blake held up his left hand to Leo and pointed to his empty ring finger, and Leo hung his head, deflating like a leaky air mattress. Once we were all back home and our physical baggage was unpacked, we figured it was time to unload our emotional baggage as well.

There is no right way to dismantle a family. I've always been direct and blunt about the hard facts of life with my children, so Blake and I called a family meeting and had the girls come into the living room, the same room where we'd unwrapped countless Christmas and birthday presents, watched hours of movies together, and shared the little moments that built our lives. Looking at their faces as their new reality dawned on them and their shields of denial shattered made me wish I was a better liar, a softer person.

"Dad and I have something we need to share with you," I started quickly before I lost my courage. "We are getting divorced."

I was completely thrown by Amara's response. I expected to be hit with a barrage of logistical questions. Where will everyone live? When will we see Dad? Do we have to go to court? I was not expecting wailing and declarations of despair.

"What are the kids at school going to think?" Amara sobbed through a flood of tears. "They will shun me. This is humiliating!"

Sophie rescued my meticulous planned responses. "Does this mean we have to move?" she angrily demanded.

Cecilia had decided this shit show would carry on without her having to witness it and simply wandered off.

Once Amara pulled herself back from her tween ledge of anguish, we got into the details. No, we were not moving, but yes, things would be very different. Blake and I had made a deal. He got the house, I got the kids.

He didn't want to sell the house because the market hadn't bounced back, but also had no intentions of living in it because he'd be in North Dakota for work. I wanted to give the kids stability for as long as possible, so we agreed that he'd rent it to me, making sure my rent would be lower than what I'd be able to find elsewhere in the area. I'd also deduct his half of daycare and other expenses from the rent. It was supposed to be a win-win for everyone.

Sophie was still skeptical of this grand plan until I told her about the best part of this whole debacle. Now that Blake was vacating the premises, we would no longer need a computer room, which meant every child could have their own bedroom door to slam in the face of an irritating sibling. Sophie would finally get her own room! Behold, the silver lining!

The following ten months were, in many ways, some of the best days of my life. There were hard moments and struggles, but oh my heart, there were so many hours of joy and bliss. Amara, Sophie, and Cecilia were all officially at an age where I no longer had to do everything for them, but instead, began to do so much *with* them. When they're babies fresh to this world, humans are so needy and demanding, parents have to do everything for them, and the process of shifting those duties to the individual child is a long and arduous one.

A perfect example is playing games. When children are young, playing a game with them is teaching them not only how to play the game, but how to conduct themselves with other humans. Now that Amara was eleven years old, Sophie was edging to a solid eight, and Cea was past trying to eat small pieces of whatever, it was absolutely glorious. We turned every Wednesday into game night! We played Blockus, Citadels, Chess, and a few simpler games with Cecilia. The trash talk was epic, the giggles contagious, and the battles often so ferocious that a win was worthy of boasting. Yes, I lorded it over an eleven-year-old when I kicked her ass at Sorry! Didn't even feel bad, either. Turnabout is fair play.

Reading was another area that had evolved from daily recitation into a beautiful exchange of ideas. I've always been an avid reader, and I tried to share my love of the written language with the girls from the moment they emerged from the womb. Our nightly bedtime routine involved me going from youngest to eldest and reading with them before they inevitably fell asleep in a pile of books.

Cecilia was still in the cocoon of being read to from picture books. She didn't care she couldn't read yet, she simply loved flipping through the pages. In the months preceding her death, she somehow acquired a paperback copy of Hunter S. Thompson's *Fear and Loathing on the Campaign Trail*. She loved that book, carried it everywhere, even slept with it like it was a stuffed animal. Cecilia would open it up and "read" detailed stories that she concocted as she flipped through the pages. I think she was mostly enamored with the cover art of a big dragon. In fact, most of her stories involved a dragon that would fly in and rescue a little girl. She'd corner me and crawl into my lap, then open the book to a random page. Her tiny finger would run along the text, and she would describe a fearsome dragon burning his foes to ash but sweetly protecting a princess. How I miss her pretty voice.

Sophie, my artist, had discovered the world of graphic novels. We'd take turns reading out loud the *Bone* series by Jeff Smith, or *Courtney Crumrin* by Ted Naifeh. It was a challenge to find these hybrid books that blended art with literature yet were still age appropriate. But it was all worth it to watch her soak it up. Her eyes devoured the brush lines and prose as they came together to paint a perfect story.

Despite being the resident brainiac, Amara was never that into reading fiction for the fun of it. Left to her own devices, she'd gravitate towards college Algebra or science textbooks, not what I considered bedtime material. She did discover the beauty of audio books during her short life and would listen to the *Eragon* series by Christopher Paolini while copying out the mathematical formulas in the college textbooks she hoarded. I was thrilled when she found *The Sisters Grimm* by Michael Buckley and bought her every copy as it became available. We read *The Hunger Games* by Suzanne Collins to each other one chapter at a time. The story is set in a dystopian future where children are selected via a lottery system to compete in games that can only be won by surviving.

"Why do they take the children?" Amara once asked me. "Why not the parents?"

"Because the worst thing you can do to someone is take their children away," I explained. "Losing your child is a worse punishment than losing your own life."

Now I know how true that is.

For the first month of our official separation, Blake's and my unraveling was slow but steady. We got the paperwork filed for the divorce, and he took most of his belongings out of the house while I stored the rest in the basement. Blake showed for his weekends with the girls and brought friends or family with him to help. I wasn't surprised he needed this assistance, as he was completely unaccustomed to being primary caregiver for them. But I was shocked when Blake became jealous and possessive.

By this point, I'd started dating a guy named Duncan from my hometown. While I wasn't ready to be involved with anyone that would be around a lot, I was incredibly lonely, so I'd allowed him to seduce me via Facebook messages. This relationship was ideal for me, as he was over 500 miles away. The majority of our romance played out via text messages and emails, a few weekend rendezvous thrown in to keep things exciting. I told Blake about what I was doing but refused to give him the details he wanted, and he became fixated on Duncan. Even though the relationship petered out after six months and I started to date other men, Blake never let go of Duncan as a target for his hate.

Blake's first official weekend with the girls was Labor Day, 2011. I'd made arrangements to go to Milwaukee to meet some friends for Pearl Jam's 20th anniversary concert. This was my first experience with his bouts of "robo-calling," as I later called it.

First, he called to tell me the girls were doing well. When it was obvious he wasn't calling to relate any parental information, I ended the call and set some boundaries. He then called me ten times in a row. I let them all go to voicemail. Then, he started calling mutual friends of ours, telling some story about me going missing. They started frantically calling me. Finally, I called Scott, a friend of Blake's.

"Scott, what the hell is going on?" I shouted through my phone. "Blake is being bizarre. He won't stop calling me, and he's calling people up and telling them I'm missing!"

"What do you expect, you broke his heart," Scott said.

I took a deep breath. "Is someone there watching the kids while he is going off the rails?"

"Yes, the kids are fine," he said and ended the call.

I chalked it up to the adjustment of separating, the reality of divorce settling in.

Blake had a couple more weekends with the kids before he shipped out to North Dakota and those were less dramatic. I was hopeful that he'd stay connected to the kids via phone calls, Skyping, and by texting photos. I even set up a Facebook page for the girls so that Blake and his family could stay up-to-date on their latest shenanigans without having to go through my page. That normalcy lasted a month.

I'd sent Blake pictures of the girls in their Halloween costumes. Amara was dressed as a bat, Sophie as a stunning Cleopatra, and Cecilia as a 60s go-go girl.

He called me sobbing, saying it all hurt too much, so he wasn't going to have anything to do with the kids anymore.

"You need help," I snarled into the phone while hiding in the closet. "Get a therapist and suck it up. This isn't about you anymore; it's about what's best for your children."

"I can't do this," he said. "I started crying in the grocery store."

"I'll stop the pictures until you can process this more, but you can't cut them off! They deserve better than that!"

But no, he was true to his word. He didn't speak to them for months, distancing himself from being their father. If one of the girls answered the phone when he tried calling, he'd just hang up.

I found a therapist for Amara and Sophie to help with this rejection. Amara loved it and found talk therapy to be incredibly beneficial. Sophie, not so much.

"So what do you think, Soph?" I asked her after her second session.

She gave me one of her classic glares. "What's the point?" she said. "It's just talking. Talking won't make him answer the phone or visit. It's just blah-blah-blah."

I racked my brain for something that might help her and came up with Aikido Korean Martial Arts. I thought maybe if she could turn her emotional turmoil into a physical force, it'd help her process things her own way. Worst case scenario, I figured, she could break some boards instead of internalizing that anger. And it did really help her. She was able to gain her yellow belt before she died.

For Thanksgiving that year, I took the girls to Illinois with the understanding that Blake would come to the house to clear out the last of his things. He stayed for a few days according to my neighbor Beth, who I'd enlisted to keep an eye on everything. I became increasingly nervous as I drove home as Beth continued to text me, telling me he was still there. He left without incident, or any furniture, about an hour before we pulled in. I was relieved to find the cat unharmed, and only a faint scent of crazy left.

The next hurdle was winter break. According to the plan, he'd stay with the girls for the entire break to celebrate Christmas and New Year's. During the weeks leading up to the holidays, I was hopeful he'd pull it together. They really missed him. I know that isn't logical. I assumed that because he was so minimally involved in their lives for the majority of the time that his absence wouldn't phase them. I was so wrong. I guess those few minutes of attention here and there added up to something that was more than the nothing they were getting. It just goes to show that even a barely there dad is better than a totally gone dad. When it became apparent that he wouldn't be following through on his promise, I took the kids to Springfield.

It was fantastic, unlike the Christmas of 2008. My parents and I had patched things up slowly and steadily over the last three years. The girls tied us together. There was no way I was going to keep them from their grandparents no matter how angry and hurt I was. I made it work for Amara, Sophie, and Cea. My brother Jack wasn't as motivated to reconnect with me. We were both motivated to keep the peace, though. Instead of fighting when we were forced to share space, we just pretended the other was a ghost that could only be communicated with via a medium. The girls and I spent the week with my parents and had a traditional Stout Christmas Eve dinner of Caesar salad, crab bisque, and fried shrimp. Christmas morning, we unstuffed stockings and passed around gifts. That day, we joined forces with my BFF Iris and her children for a Cajun Christmas feast of gumbo and greens. Sophie, whose birthday is two days after Christmas, had always been slightly neglected in that way only kids born during the holy holiday season can understand, but we made it up as best we could. Grandma and Grandpa made a special dinner and lavished her with love and gifts.

A few days later, Iris hosted Sophie's last friends birthday party, and it was everything she wanted and more. She handmade a snowman piñata, filled dozens of eggs with confetti, and set up a jump-roping contest. The weather was unseasonably warm, so we were able to do the egg hunt outside. Sophie cackled the loudest while smashing the confetti-filled eggs on my head. All of the kids had a blast, and I'll never be able to repay Iris for those precious memories.

We wrapped up 2011, then bid our farewells and headed north to welcome 2012. A court date had been set for the divorce. Monday, January 9th would find us standing before a judge testifying to our respective inabilities to stand by our vows.

But before that, the first of two speeding tickets.

Cea and I were rocking out to a Beastie Boys' song on the way to daycare that rough Monday morning when life decided that getting divorced wasn't enough misfortune for the day. River Falls is a small town, and like most small towns, has its well-established speed traps. This one is on a short stretch that's on a downward slope with a 25 MPH limit as you glide past a car dealership that easily conceals a squad car. I was clocked at 36 MPH.

The officer who so kindly wrote out my ticket would, months later, be the same officer to take my statement as I recalled Blake's threat to harm the girls.

When I got to court, I was a sloppy bag of emotions, while Blake had begun talking to the girls again, giving him a bit of a reprieve from my simmering rage. We were able to have a few conversations that didn't end with me calling him an "asshole" or an "insane douche bag," which is to say, there was progress.

The hearing itself was simple and straightforward due in part to the lack of lawyers. The presiding judge showed some concern that Blake was getting the shit-end of the deal because of our unique housing arrangement, but otherwise it went through without a hitch. As I was exiting the courtroom, I was felled by a sledgehammer of grief.

I broke down sobbing uncontrollably. It was all just so fucking sad. Blake hugged me until I calmed down the waterworks, and then said, "I think we earned a drink, don't you?"

The next thing I knew we were at a small table at a local establishment, a shot of whiskey in front of each of us and a decade of marriage behind. We toasted to the things we did right (our beautiful children) and the things we did wrong (mostly each other). We shared laughs and cried a bit, then left to carry on with the business of living.

I headed home to greet Amara and Sophie as they got off the bus. I prepped them for our unexpected dinner guest as I cut up veggies and marinated chicken.

Blake was running his own errands and gathering Cecilia from day-care, and so came the day's second speeding ticket. He was pulled over in the exact same speed trap I was, for breaking the speed limit by exactly the same speed. Neither of us had gotten a speeding ticket in years. It was a strange coincidence that has stuck with me for years. I'm not sure what the universe was trying to tell me.

I'd like to blame the tickets for upsetting my emotional basket and causing me to make a bunch of sloppy choices for the rest of the day. But I can't, not really. As much as I was done with Blake, my feelings for him and the life we'd built together were not going to simply evaporate by signing a document.

I'm drawing a blank for the hours between the drink and dinner. I know Blake picked up his speeding ticket and Cecilia before coming back to spend time with the kids. He ate dinner with us at home, then took Sophie to her Akido class, then brought her home after class was done and helped put the kids to bed. He did most of the tucking that night, maybe trying to make up a bit for all the times he wasn't present for them. Or, maybe learning their habits to set the stage for a future evil deed.

Once the girls were settled, he brought out a bottle of tequila. One of those fancy ones that looks like a crystal skull. I popped in a few CDs to play on rotate and sat down across from him at the kitchen table.

The table that had been my first adult purchase, the impetus for the party that ended with Blake declaring his brutal love for me. The table where we had blown out birthday candles, dyed Easter eggs, corrected homework, and played countless games of cribbage on. The table that had witnessed so much of our lives now watched as we shared our last drinks together.

Tequila shots were consumed. Emotional shots were volleyed. Pot shots were taken with good humor. I remember a little laughing and a lot of reminiscing. Then the words of Jessica Lea Mayfield poured out of the speakers, and we were drowning in the chords of "Kiss Me Again."

I got up swaying a bit, to the music of course, not the tequila. I turned it up and sang along, badly and loudly. Then he was there in front of me, taking me in those strong arms that made me so weak in the boundaries.

Then, he did what he always did well…kissed me. By the time "You've Won Me Over" ended, he'd carried me up to the bedroom. We didn't make love, because that was buried too deep to dredge up. We had sad, awkward, frustrating sex, and then he left.

I curled up and fell asleep, satisfied that I'd done nothing right all day and now it had ended.

Neither of us harbored any delusions that our divorce day reminiscing would result in a reconciliation. Blake went back to Minot and slowly stopped talking to the girls again. I settled back into the work of raising three very busy people. Everything fell into a comfortable routine again.

Amara and Sophie were still going to troop meetings. Sophie had Akido weekly and Amara's spring soccer season was just around the corner. Cecilia, only four, was not in any organized activities of her own yet. I was at my organizational limits juggling the older girls' schedules and simply couldn't add another ball. I thought I had years yet to get her into a sport or club of her choosing. At the very least, I was able to provide her with some amazing music experiences before she left this world.

Cecilia was my musical buddy. The other girls enjoyed music and would join in on an impromptu dance party, but Cea was the real connoisseur. I was always playing The Current, the local public radio station, in the car and at home. She continued to meticulously critique most of the songs. "I like the beat in this one but not the words," she would pipe up from the backseat on the way to daycare. We would spend hours looking up artists on YouTube and fall down digital rabbit holes of indie music.

I still feel incredibly blessed that I was able to take all three girls to see The Portland Cello Project and Emily Wells play live at the Cedar Cultural Center in Minneapolis. They even got an autograph and a picture with Emily Wells.

The best concert was when I took them to see Cloud Cult play at the UW-River Falls Finals Bash. There could not have been a better concert experience for my complicated creatures. Cloud Cult had two artists on stage with them while they performed. The artists painted on canvases that were attached to a contraption that allowed them to be spun in all directions during the show. Sophie was enraptured by paintings coming to formation before her eyes. Amara, ever the engineer, promised to build her one of those easels. Cecilia just rocked out!

The girls and I really enjoyed what we didn't know would be our last six months together. Amara got more into baking and cooking. Sophie's art was celebrated in the district-wide art show. And Cecilia kept us all on our toes. We played together, grew together, fought and cried together; we really *lived* together. Oh, how I miss them.

Those last six months I shared them more than I now wish I had. Grandpa Leo and Step-Grandma Dolores stepped up to take the girls once a month for a weekend to make up for all the visits their dad missed. My parents took them for the whole month of June after school was out so they could attend their favorite camps in Springfield and get spoiled. I know the girls treasured those times with their elders. It is only my selfish heart that regrets those days I didn't know I was sacrificing.

For a couple months, I'd gotten a reprieve from Blake. The robo-calling had stopped and our conversations were few and far between. But now, I'm no longer positive of the exact timeline which came first—the car accident or the death threats.

I remember him one day calling me in a confessional mood. He said he'd been drinking excessively and rear-ended another car. He bragged to me that thanks to his medications masking his intoxication, the police officer who came to document the wreck didn't even think to test his sobriety. Fate would have it that this officer was the same one who also was called to do a welfare check on Blake after he told me he wanted to torture me.

In early March, I was diligently entering case notes in my cube that I shared with two other social workers when I saw Blake's number pop up on my work cell. I answered the phone while dodging into the empty conference room for some privacy. I do not recall how the conversation started but will never forget how it ended.

His disembodied voice slithered into my ear. "I have been having this thought a lot lately," he said. "Sometimes, I think about this six times a day. I imagine driving down there, tying you up and making you choose which kid I kill. Then, making you watch while I do it."

"You can't just say things like that, Blake!" I yelled back. "What the fuck is wrong with you? I am calling the police. This is serious. You need help."

While most people may not take something like that seriously, I was trained to do so. I hung up and did exactly what I said I'd do. I called the police, and they had me come down to the station to make an official statement. I begged them to have the Minot police do a 72-hour hold on Blake, convinced this was the result of him mismanaging his medication and drinking too much. An officer went to Blake's apartment and determined that he was not a threat to himself or others.

Shocked by Blake's behavior, I went to the St. Croix County Victim's Advocates office to get information about orders for protection and harassment restraining orders. I could have spent a pretty penny and petitioned for a restraining order for myself, but my case was flimsy and he still had rights as a parent. I would have had to take him to family court to legally bar him from having contact with the kids. The fact that he was several states away and no longer had a vehicle helped me feel safer. I was planning on taking Amara, Sophie, and Cecilia to Springfield for spring break anyway, and decided to leave a couple days early to put that much more distance between us and their imbalanced father.

Over the next month, I talked with family and friends, and got their opinion on Blake's odd behavior. Blake and I had a few conversations, and he seemed to have reigned it in. I was hopeful he'd turned a corner and was dialing back on the booze, at least.

We still had one last loose end to tie up from the divorce. He had to refinance the mortgage and get my name removed from the deed. One night in late April, he called to say he was in town to deal with house stuff.

I was skeptical, but he pointed out that we were working with a smaller local credit union. I conceded the point and asked if he needed anything from me.

"Actually," he said, "I was hoping I could come over and see the girls."

The hairs on the back of my neck went up. "They're sleeping!" I said. "It's after ten o'clock at night."

"I just want to peek in on them," he said. "They're so peaceful when they are asleep."

"No. They do not get anything out of you sneaking in to see them sleeping. It's creepy and it's late. If you sincerely want to see them, we can set something up for tomorrow in a public place."

I offered this option thinking it would be good for him to see the kids, that it would be a safe baby step towards healing. He agreed, and we made arrangements to meet at a restaurant in Hudson, Wisconsin the next evening, about 15 minutes from the house. The plan was that I would hand the girls off in front of the Winzer Stube, then meet them a couple hours later at the public park by the river.

We got there first and as I stood trying to peer through the glass door to see if he was inside. He came up behind me and said, "Hi."

I jumped about twenty feet straight up and yelped.

"Do I scare you, Jess?" he asked with a smirk.

I didn't have to answer because the girls mobbed him with hugs, screaming "We miss you so much!"

I said good-bye to the kids and reiterated that I'd meet them at the park in two hours. The visit went well, according to the kids. The hand-off back was uneventful and I left feeling better.

Looking back on it now, I believe in my very bones that if I'd let him come to the house the night before he would've killed us all. At that point, I had no knowledge of Blake's attempts to locate and pay someone to slaughter us or the deadly plans he whispered to his cousin. I wouldn't know any of those details until the trial. In retrospect, he learned a lot on that trip. He found out that he would have to make amends and earn back my trust if he was going to get the access he needed. And he spent the next two months doing just that.

Blake said all the things I needed to hear, then backed up his words with actions I needed to see. He called my parents and apologized. He began talking to the girls on a regular basis and Skyping them. He told me he quit drinking, and that he had his medications adjusted. He started making real plans to spend time with the girls and didn't balk when I told him I wanted his dad involved with the visits. He told me he'd set up a Match.com account and was starting to date again. All these things seemed like evidence to me that he'd hit rock bottom and was now crawling out of his pit of despair, trying to make the best of things.

It was now late June, and Amara, Sophie, and Cea were in Springfield wrapping up their summer vacation. I missed them and couldn't wait to get them back home. Blake and I had a long Skype session, talking about the girls and about our lives. He looked good. Healthy and sober. He sounded sane and purposeful. Yet again, I was charmed by his mask.

Chapter Twelve

A Headstone
and a Possibly Possessed Tree

Dearest Departed Daughters,

Picking out your headstone sucked.

I resented having to bury you at all. I wanted you here with me, complaining about sharing a bathroom and fighting over what theme it should be. I know you are probably more than a little irritated with me that I am making you share one headstone. It's bad enough that I incinerated your bodies and mixed them together, and now you don't even get your own hunks of rock to be memorialized by. Well, love butts, life wasn't fair and neither is death.

There are so many choices that go into picking out a headstone and a burial plot. What color stone? What font for the names? What images and symbols to incorporate? What sacred ground to place them in? Like every other step in this process, I did not do it alone. Grandpa Rhett came with me. He watched his baby try to bury her babies. He stayed as the walls I had built around the anger began to crumble and the rage seeped through the cracks. I know it took more out of him than it did me. But we're Stouts, so we pulled it together and got through it.

I used a local business that is family owned and operated called Melgard Monument. They have been around since 1888, but even with all of that history and knowledge of how short life can be, your deaths rocked them to their cores. Korey Melgard, one of our neighbors, made the process as easy as he could. He told me about how all three of you would play with his children, and reminded me of how many lives you had touched that I was unaware of. He connected me with an amazing artist who was willing to turn my pain into a totem that others could witness and touch. I needed to create something solid and enduring to remind the world you were here. Something tangible that could never be denied. A focal point for those who knew you to come to and pour their grief into, and then be able to leave with just the love left in their hearts from knowing you.

Pink would have been too sweet for my sassy girls, white too easily stained by this world, and black is my color to hold inside. There were so few things that all three of you agreed about, but you all loved the color blue. So, Grandpa and I chose a blue grey stone from India. The artist was inspired by the tattoo on my chest, and placed an owl's head over three hearts, each holding your names and vitals in cursive. Only one of you learned to write that way.

The base of the stone has a quote on it: "Life is eternal; and love is immortal; and death is only a horizon; and a horizon is nothing save the limit of our sight." It's by Rossiter W. Raymond. I debated putting your last name on the headstone, but I couldn't bring myself to allow that much of your murderer into this space. I needed something to remind me that you were not gone, just changed.

The back is adorned with an anonymously-written poem. It's meant to remind me of what I need to do, even if I don't want to do it.

You can shed tears that she is gone,
or you can smile because she has lived.
You can close your eyes and pray that she'll come back,
or you can open your eyes and see all she's left.
Your heart can be empty because you can't see her,
or you can be full of the love you shared.
You can turn your back on tomorrow and live yesterday,
or you can be happy for tomorrow because of yesterday.
You can remember her only that she is gone,
or you can cherish her memory and let it live on.
You can cry and close your mind,
be empty and turn your back.
Or you can do what she'd want:
smile, open your eyes, love and go on.
All that was left was picking a place to plant you, as they say.

I chose Greenwood Cemetery because of the memories. I thought you would appreciate being across the street from your elementary school. I also remembered that time when Amara was at soccer practice and Sophie was at her troop meeting, so Cea and I enjoyed a stroll through the cemetery in the meantime. She asked if she would be buried at Greenwood when she died. I assured you, baby, that you'd live a long life and die far away from this little town, that I wouldn't live long enough to see where. Sometimes when I drive past, I pretend to see us strolling through the tombstones hand and hand.

The graveyard keepers allowed me to pick a plot that was in an area that was not yet occupied. I wanted you girls to stick out like a sore thumb, to beckon the eyes of people driving by. The expanse is bordered by maple trees, so I had my pick of trees to tuck you in under. I examined each possibility closely. Looking for prime climbing material. Searching for a resemblance to the tree in Grandma and Grandpa's backyard in Springfield that all three of you scaled as soon as you could reach the lowest branch. I think I found, if not the perfect tree, then at least the best pick of the bunch.

That's where we buried a third of your ashes. We put them in a beautiful handmade wooden urn that's meant to rot and release you back into the dirt, back where we all come from.

I rarely visit. I chose that place for others, a place for memories of you to be shared. A conduit for the love you gave while you were able to give it. I wanted it to be a place that your friends could come to without me needing to act as a gatekeeper. But like many things in life, it's become more than I intended.

That tree I picked has a stubborn streak. It refuses to shed its leaves until the other trees have stripped to their skivvies. It's not a subtle display of rebellion, but a bright, bold, blatant defiance of nature's order. I don't know if it was always that way, or if your souls corrupted it. I don't care. It's a beautiful sight.

I don't need proof of your souls reaching out from the great beyond. I am haunted by your absence and comforted by the light your energy has left behind. I do appreciate that the tree shows to the world that sometimes it's hard to let go. I would love to hear what Amara, my budding scientist and declared atheist, would say. I can hear her subtle inhale as she begins her botany lesson. "Well, actually there is a logical explanation for this anomaly..." I am sure Sophie, the philosopher, would have an argument that the power of feelings affected the tree's behavior. Little Cea would tell us we're all missing the point, that all that's important is it's a very pretty tree.

Others have shared stories of what they feel at your grave. They say it's evidence of you girls reaching out from the horizon to remind us that you're still here. I honor these stories. I respect the truths they hold. I do not need to debate or dissect them to prove the validity of their claims. It doesn't matter. I can hold those truths in my mind and in my heart, and let them be united and separate all at once. I don't need proof that the three of you continue to affect this world, because as long as I continue to move forward, I carry you with me. I, like that stubborn tree, refuse to let go.

Anyway, it is a very pretty tree.

Kisses,
Mama

Chapter Thirteen

Going Out In Style

They don't teach you about the logistics of surviving this type of thing. There is no manual called *Mourning Your Murdered Children* or *Getting Justice for Dummies*. There's not even a pamphlet for the *Practicalities of Grieving and Criminal Trials*. No directions are provided for rebuilding lives that are gutted to the core like this. Some may counter by saying that babies don't come with a manual, either, and most folks manage to figure out that life event just fine. Joyful additions to the world elicit tons of advice—solicited or otherwise—while tragic subtractions only beget awkward silence.

Even so, time wasn't waiting for me to figure it out. There were so many choices to be made, and bodies to bury.

I was in the "war room" at the one hotel that was as close to a home base as I was going to have for the foreseeable future. We were putting together displays for the memorial service a few days after the girls had died.

My sister had made thousands of copies of photos that featured the girls, and Olivia, Iris, and Dawn were using them to put collages together on three huge boards. (Dawn and I had long since forgotten that weird night when Blake got us drunk.) Meanwhile, I was spinning like a top, trying to see every image of the girls I could, my eyes devouring faces my lips could never touch again. I wanted to bury myself in that picture pile and never come out. Instead, I had to go shopping.

My wardrobe was still under the surveillance of law enforcement, and I was with it enough to know that showing up to your kids' funeral naked was frowned upon. So, we went to a fancy dress shop in Woodbury, Minnesota. My brother, Jack, had brought me to buy a mourning gown with all the requisite accessories of earrings and a necklace, or at least make sure I had matching shoes.

As I rifled through the racks, it dawned on me that I'd never be the mother of the bride now. I'd never watch Amara marry whoever managed to distract her long enough to fall in love. I wouldn't witness Sophie's multitude of spouses walk her down ever more extravagant aisles—trust me, that child would've left a wake of broken hearts before finding someone who wouldn't stifle her passion. And Cea, and Cea, and Cea... She was so little, I didn't know who she would've grown up to be yet.

Fuck. I started sobbing again, right there in the store. I made a mental note to remind myself to start carrying tissues.

I don't remember choosing a dress, heels, or jewelry, but I still recall the look on the saleslady's face as she figured out who I was, and what I'd lost. Her desire to hug me and ward off the evil that lingered around me became plain as day. It was a complex chemical reaction that I'd become accustomed to.

My brother rushed me out the door, whispering, "Quick, before she calls the media."

At that time, I'd been maintaining a mostly television-free home for a decade and the only news I consumed was via NPR. So, I was wholly unprepared when the story of three little girls being slaughtered by their father spread across the globe.

Amara, Sophie, and Cecilia's beautiful faces graced the pages of newspapers in every state of our nation. A shard of my broken heart swelled to see them smiling at me from television screens and hear praises from strangers. But that disintegrated when the next image shown was of their murderer.

At one point during the first days of despair, I asked why I was being moved around so much.

Dawn explained, "So the vultures don't catch you and plaster you across the internet."

"I am a sobbing mess, why would anyone want to see that?" I responded while blowing my nose.

"Oh, honey," Dawn said. "That's exactly what they want to see."

I managed to avoid any direct contact with the professional media for almost a year. One perk of being homeless is that the press can't find ya. But they still did their best to track me down by calling my workplace, friends, and family. One of my greatest defenders was my Uncle Stone who volunteered to be the family spokesman, the stoic face of our sorrow so we were free to rant and rave without an audience. He was the best pick for the job, even if hadn't volunteered. As my mom's oldest brother, he was accustomed to keeping it cool when everyone else was losing their temper.

However, media in modern times is no longer a single beast but a many-headed hydra. And most often the head with the fiercest bite is social media.

I had my Facebook account and the account I created for the girls. After they died, both pages were flooded with friend requests, which I dumbly accepted without thought. It didn't take long for pictures of the girls to be lifted from these sites and spread across the interwebs like spilled ink. I shut down my personal account and handed over the girls' account to a steadier hand. Posts from both would be scrutinized by law enforcement during the investigation, and some found their way into immortality via the court transcripts.

A lesson I will forever carry with me is that once anything is released onto the internet it is forever out of your control. A woman that I had never met created a Facebook page for the girls called TriAngels. It started with good intentions but quickly morphed into something akin to emotional vampirism. This person did not know Amara, Sophie, Cecilia, or even me. While many of our biggest supporters were strangers when the girls died, this woman started presenting herself as a part of a family she'd never met.

It's a fine line that's easy to cross from memorialization to profiteering. I try to be mindful of crossing that boundary myself. I want to share Amara, Sophie, and Cea with the world, and want their stories told and for my journey to bring solace to others. That's why I wrote this memoir, after all. I do not want to exploit our tragedy. (The woman did take down the page after a few firm requests.)

I couldn't bring myself to read any of the articles or watch the news reports for years. I didn't even check the weather and relied on good ol' word of mouth to let me know Obama had secured another term that year.

My avoidance of the news was likely one of the things that allowed me to survive those first years without my girls. It gave me time to heal and be in a place to read those articles, and all of the misinformation inside of them, without feeling the paper cut stings of a thousand little lies. Once I did get around to reading some of the articles, I was able to blow off most of the inaccuracies.

But there was one thing repeated over and over that still chaps my ass.

For whatever reason, the journalists felt the need to say, in a million little ways, that I was "away" from home at the time of the murders. Like I was on vacation, or off on a jaunt. I was working. I was at work supporting my family. It's not that hard to say the "ex-wife" —also an interesting choice instead of "mother" —was working when her children were killed. Instead, the implication I was just away seemed necessary to the droves of journalists.

The words used were technically correct but insidious. I wasn't in the house when my home was destroyed. I was elsewhere, and then I was nowhere for a very, very long time.

Home is where your heart is, they say. Well, I had no heart left after what Blake did and no walls to call my own.

I was bouncing from hotel to hotel for weeks, but it felt like years. At some point, I was brought back to a room somewhere in St. Paul. I stumbled in. I'd been in a bar, drinking and publicly bawling, that much I know. Then suddenly, I was being tackled by a small, aggressive woman who wanted to shove a pill down my throat.

"Mom! Stop! I've been drinking!" I yelled, shaking my head back and forth. "I don't think I should be taking any drugs."

"I just don't want you to hurt, Jessica," she pleaded. "Take it so you can sleep."

"It's okay, it's okay," I lied as I rocked her back and forth before finally crawling into an empty bed.

Sometime the next day, or maybe it was two days later, I was back in the war room. My uncles had surrounded me in a protective huddle. A couple of them were lawyers, all heartbroken. Someone from the prosecution team was filling us in—Uncle Sam wanted them to push for it to be a federal case, seeing as Blake crossed state lines. Wisconsin doesn't have the death penalty, but the good ol' U.S.A. sure does.

"No, I want him to live a long, miserable life in a cage," I said. "Death is a mercy he does not deserve."

The conversation moved to Blake's public defender and how skilled he was.

"That's good," I said. "The last thing we need is for him to get a second trial due to an incompetent defense."

I was in another hotel room on someone's computer sometime later searching for music for the girls' memorial. Somehow, I ended up on the website of the band named Cloud Cult and my soul shattered. I laid down on the hotel bed with the laptop glow lighting the darkened room, listening to their heartrending songs of loss.

I sent them an email thanking them for their beautiful music, telling them how much the girls had enjoyed the concert they'd attended, not expecting a response. Frankly, not expecting anything from the universe again.

Craig and Connie Minowa, the core of Cloud Cult, quickly wrote me back. Many of their songs come from coping with the death of their own son, Kaidin, who passed when he was just two years old.

They soon offered to play at the memorial and mourn with me for my baby girls. I was blown away.

Not that I can remember which songs they played, or what it was even like to meet them in person that first time. Any moments of clarity were mere pinpricks in the mantle of numbness my brain had wrapped me inside of. I was utterly useless.

Around me, an army of family and friends did the work of organizing, coordinating, and making decisions while they grieved, too. I floated around, piping in now and then with vague requests and poignant declarations. Mostly, I tried to survive one hour at a time.

I drank too much, and for once in my life, ate too little. All meaning and structure had been ripped from my life. I was in no place for introspection. Looking to my own wounds was not yet within my abilities. So, instead of looking inwards, I tried to look out into the ocean of mourning surrounding me. I knew I couldn't staunch my pain, but maybe I could do a little something to embrace others.

The girls and I were active Unitarians, and I realized their deaths were not only my tragedy. The whole community was traumatized. So, I asked many different denominations to be involved in the memorial service.

One of the biggest hurdles was the site of the service. The Catholic church was the only venue even remotely big enough for the expected crowd, but their beliefs couldn't accommodate having other religious leaders practicing under their roof. The various Lutheran churches were too small to consider and equally dominant within their domains. Fortunately, the local golf club was a place where everyone could come together no matter what they practiced.

With that taken care of, I pulled it together long enough to pick out a meaningful charity for each of my daughters.

Amara's was the River Falls Food Shelf, not only because she was my baker. When we'd gone through a rough patch and had to rely on food stamps and the local food shelf, she was old enough to be aware of our struggles. She saw a flyer at school for a program coordinated between the school district and the local food shelf for children whose families needed help. Independent of any adult direction, she signed up. I couldn't think of a better program to support in her honor.

Choosing for Cecilia Lee was the easiest. It was our favorite source of music: 89.3 FM "The Current," the Twin Cities' public radio station, one of the best around. A typical hour-long set would start off with the Beastie Boys, followed by Tom Waits, then Johnny Cash melding into a Frank Sinatra standard before segueing into The Lumineers. And yes, they're the only radio station I have ever heard play the tUnE-yArDs, one of her favorites. We'd listen to The Current to and from daycare every day, and Cea would sit in her carseat yelling out praises and criticisms for every song that came on, so there was no better charity for her memory to support. Wherever Cecilia is now, she's most certainly dancing.

For Sophie's charity, I chose the local library. I figured if any institution deserved extra financial support in her name, this was the one. I can't remember how many late and lost book fees I paid over the years because of her addiction to reading. And so, every time a new book was purchased in Sophie's honor, a memorial sticker was placed on the inside cover.

There was one book called *Have You Ever Seen a Smack of Jellyfish?* by Sarah Asper-Smith. It's an alphabet book about collective nouns. It starts out innocently enough. But three letters in, it mentions something about the plural form of crows, a murder. Someone apparently took offense on my behalf and complained to the librarian. The library pulled the book and removed the sticker, and later apologized to me.

I explained it was in no way offensive to me, and that Sophie would find the whole drama deliciously ridiculous. Even now, I can hear her cackling about it. The book was allowed back in rotation but has lost its Sophie branding.

What an odd thing it is to memorialize three very different children at the same time.

People poured in from all over the country to give me their condolences, but there was so much going on that it all barely skimmed the surface of my awareness. Candlelight vigils, parking lot fund raisers, Facebook pages, memorial bracelets, more praying than I could ever fathom. The quantity of support was only surpassed by its endurance. The flood of love surged during those first hours and days, but the rain came down steady for years. The community came forward and picked our family up, and in some ways, ten years later, still hasn't put us down.

But this wasn't my party. It wasn't about me. The goddess knows I wish I could have been the one on the pyre, but I was just there to bear witness to their lives. Funerals were attended by those who loved the deceased, and many of those who loved them were not my friends. Some were already on the path to becoming my enemies.

A theme would emerge, one that would test my character again and again, was that Amara, Sophie, and Cea were also part of Blake's family. His parents, siblings, aunts, uncles, and cousins all loved the girls, and my beautiful girls had loved them, too. I did not have room to sympathize with them as they mourned their own loss. They grappled with the girls' deaths as they also dealt with the loss of their son/brother/nephew/friend, who they thought they *knew* and had caused their pain.

At the memorial service, I pulled together enough decency to make sure they weren't excluded, as we all wept for our lost loves. For many, the service was the last event before lines were drawn. In less than a year, many of those offering me love and strength would be advocating for the release of my children's murderer.

On the day of the memorial service, I quickly realized holding it at the local golf course was really the only viable option. Not just because it was neutral ground, but also because none of the churches were large enough to deal with the crowd. There were just so many people there.

Matt, my new beau, stood by my side the entire time. He'd only ever seen pictures and heard stories of the girls, but felt their loss and stepped into my grief without hesitation.

We'd met on Match.com, like most freshly-divorced adults had back in the day. We both lived in River Falls, but our children were different enough in age that there'd be no chance we'd bump into each other at their activities. We went on our first date on June 29th, and were instantly infatuated. When I called him from the police station to tell him not to go to the house, I never expected to see or hear from him again. Matt did a lot of soul-searching and praying, then came down to help.

And he just kept showing up.

At the service, he stood nearby as a river of people surged around me. When they threatened to carry me off, he anchored me, emotionally and physically. Matt was, of course, saddened by the death of my children, but his grief was dulled by not having known them. This helped my situation quite a bit.

While my tribe was as wounded as I was, Matt was able to attend to me without having to staunch his own bleeding as he did so. He rolled with every punch thrown at him. If a mourner hung on too long, he gently moved them forward. He shook hands with ex-boyfriends, neighbors, teachers, and old classmates. When the hugging pushed my strapless bra down far enough to risk a humiliating exposure, Matt subtlety hiked it back up. Talk about baptism by fire.

The service was beautiful and perfect. Or so I've been told. Honestly, I don't remember shit. Where true recollection should be there is just a scattering of images, snatches of words, and a vortex of sorrow.

I barely remember Cloud Cult playing, and their music breaking through my shell of grief. I recall Marvin, an ex-paratrooper who I dated briefly, making it past the first set of doors before breaking down and leaving. He and I had figured out after a few weeks that we weren't a good match, but the girls had hooked his heart nonetheless. Again and again, I'd see some of the most hardened men in my life laid low by the fate of my girls.

One of my oldest friends who I hadn't seen since before Cecilia was born had travelled cross-country with her newly-born daughter to share in my sorrow.

There was a moment I recall being outside looking at the stars, smoking a cigarette. I'm not a smoker, but that night I needed to burn something. I remember someone's aunt hugging me and saying over and over how beautiful I looked.

"I guess grief becomes me," I responded.

And become grief, I did.

In a lot of ways, because of their deaths, I've become the embodiment of mourning, grief, sorrow, and loss. When people see me and know what I've lost, and how I'm carrying on, it's what I've come to symbolize for them. My daughters' deaths didn't just destroy my family, it came to define me. I stopped being so-and-so's mom and became the mother of loss.

Chapter Fourteen

Holland, 1945

A few days after the memorial service, my dad took me to the grocery store and wandered off, leaving me alone in the aisles. I came upon the peanut butter section and began hunting for the right brand. A few years previous, I'd become a health food convert and had meticulously calculated which peanut butter was the healthiest but still consumable by small, picky people.

I stared and stared at the rows of jars and then, like lightning, it hit me. It didn't matter anymore which *fucking* peanut butter I got.

My kids were dead.

There'd be no more peanut butter and honey sandwiches, hastily made at a playground while the girls swung from the monkey bars. They'd never eat another spoonful of peanut butter between nagging about how long dinner was taking. I'd never again hold a tiny face in my hand and wipe a smear of peanut butter from a cheek before replacing it with a kiss.

And so that's how my father found me, curled up on the grocery store floor, hugging a jar of JIF with tears streaming down my face.

It's a good thing I found a therapist willing to take me on so quickly after the murders. And the universe sure was trying to balance the scales when it offered me up to Shay Marie.

In my first session with Shay, I came in weighed down by jewelry. I insisted I couldn't leave the house without wearing three of everything— three of the Amara-Sophie-Cea neon bracelets on each arm, three memorial necklaces layered around my neck, pockets bulging with trios of trinkets. For the first few appointments, Shay listened to me babble about anything and everything but the girls, waiting me out until the day I was ready. She let me live in my grief and supported me in my decision to not take any medication.

Everyone has their own journey, and every person needs to find the tools that work for them. Staying away from medication was important to me. I wasn't depressed, paranoid, or catatonic. I was mourning my children, my loss of identity, the complete upheaval of my life. I didn't want to take something that might alter my brain chemistry or, more importantly, stop me from feeling. I was not willing to risk losing the experience of joy just to avoid the gutting pain.

I'm not exaggerating when I say that I hurt every single day. Therapy with Shay didn't teach me to stop feeling the pain, but rather how to carry it, how to keep it close. Kahlil Gibran, my go-to philosopher, put it like this:

> *"Your joy is your sorrow unmasked. And the selfsame well from which your laughter rises was oftentimes filled with your tears. And how else can it be? The deeper that sorrow carves into your being, the more joy you can contain."*

It's a passage that reminds me that my joys must be as high as my sorrows are deep. I have a duty to make sure my angels' deaths are the darkest point in my life, and that every step I take out from that pitch-black moment brings more and more light into this world. I won't sacrifice an ounce of the pain that their loss causes me to risk forsaking even a mote of the love and joy Amara, Sophie, and Cecilia gave me every day of their lives.

In the meantime, before I got to this point, I had a lot of work left to do. The girls may have been dead but they were not buried, and the man who slaughtered them still needed to be brought to justice and locked away.

Breathing, eating, and speaking the occasional full sentence had returned to my arsenal, and basic survival skills seeped back into my daily routines. I couldn't deny I was still alive and would need to carry on. But while the bare minimum can be accomplished anywhere, waging war against injustice and grief requires a fortress. So, if I was going to step it up and fight the battles ahead of me I'd need a bit more stability.

All of which is to say, the pressing question was: where was I going to live?

I couldn't keep hotel hopping forever. Lucky for me, I had Sam Aritan.

Sam was a complete stranger until he'd entered my life with his offer to house my parents, and then me. He, like many others in my community, saw my tragedy and was called to help. Sam had been a local police officer when he was younger and still had many connections within the force. He reached out through those old contacts to offer my battered family refuge.

He had a very successful business that allowed him to build what was essentially a mansion in the country surrounding River Falls, and in his incredible generosity, he offered up his home as a refuge. It was just what we needed. He had a suite of rooms in the lower level that were furnished and available for habitation, while the remote locale kept media and strangers, often well-meaning but equally as often frightening, away. Sam, his long-term girlfriend, and his young son would become good friends in a very hard time.

After we'd secured a temporary residence, it was time to figure out what to do with all of the belongings still in the house. Yet again, my family stepped up and did what I wasn't capable of.

They went into what had once been a home but was now a grisly tomb. My family thought the biggest hurdle to dealing with the house would be the emotional trauma of having to spend hours in a crime scene packing up the shreds of a ruined family. So, they were rather taken aback when it was something entirely different—Blake's mother and father trying to deny them access.

I was no longer a joint owner of the property, just a tenant. And these proxy landlords didn't want us going in and taking everything. It was a dick move, for sure, but it was also illegal, as I was guaranteed access until the end of month. And those assholes were guaranteed my mother's wrath.

In the best of times, Louise had a renowned temper and penchant for creative vengeance. She uttered several vile curses, then directed the auctioneering company to take everything along with the rest of my belongings. She walked through the kitchen, opening drawers to make sure no spoon or mug was left behind.

The crew leader from Auction Services came in. "It looks like we are almost wrapped up," he said. "Anything else you can think of?"

Louise turned to him with a gleam in her eye. "Now that you mention it, take all of the appliances, too," she said. "Anything not nailed down!"

Blake's parents were not pleased when they discovered the gaps left where the washer and dryer once sat.

Two things had to happen with that house before we could move on from it. First, everything had to be taken out, and second, a professional cleaning crew had to clean up the blood.

The auctioneer company moved everything, stored it, and then after I had time to go through it, sold much of it off. I lost a lot of things in this process and, in retrospect, made a few short-sighted choices. The universe can throw some wicked curve balls. Sometimes they look like a divorce, losing a home, or even being a victim of a catastrophe. When these events come into a life, they often result in the loss of property that can be as devastating as the emotional trauma. I sum up this time in my life as "the fire". Even today, I still occasionally long for some special dish, movie, or book and think to myself, *Damn, lost that in the fire, too!*

Literal fire did destroy one thing, though.

A few days after we cleaned out the house, Leo called and asked for the small but beautifully built bedside table Blake had hand-crafted.

"Please, Jessica," he begged. "It was the one good thing he ever made."

"He destroyed the most beautiful things he ever made," I snarled back. "He destroyed the best things he'll ever do! Now, you'll just have to wait for him to make you a card in prison! I am going to take that table and smash it into a million pieces and then burn them!"

When I say I'm going to do something, I do it.

Matt graciously offered his backyard fire pit, a variety of destructive implements, and a little accelerant. It was a lovely, late summer evening that should've been spent watching children chase fireflies and eat smores. Instead, I carried the table out into the backyard for destructive catharsis.

I looked at it intently. It took Blake forever to build. When I was pregnant and waiting to give birth to Amara, I had signed him up for a furniture building class but it wouldn't be completely finished until after Cea's birth. In the fire, I took in every curve of its spindly legs, the smooth top that once held trinkets that the girls would leave by my bedside.

My parents, brother, and I took turns with a sledgehammer and an axe, smashing the wood until it splintered into tiny fragments. Then we picked up the shreds and chunks, and piled them high in the fire ring. Once a suitable pyre was constructed, my brother baptized it with a bottle of lighter fluid, and I tossed the match.

There was a beat of silence, then a great whoosh of fire being born. It burned so bright and hot. After a while, there was nothing left but a cold pile of ash.

All in all, a very cathartic experience. I highly recommend it.

The process of going through everything else was slow. I loved those girls, but damn, were they budding hoarders. So many trinkets and doodads and toys and clothes, and frankly, garbage.

I tried my best to make sure everyone had the opportunity to take something meaningful with them. I kept a third, gave a third to friends and family, and sold or donated the rest.

I regret giving up most of the books, but every single room had one or two bookcases bursting with tomes. I couldn't bear to donate them locally—I pictured friends or small children opening one to find a note written to or by the girls; little emotional time-bombs—so my sister took most of the books to a reservation in South Dakota. It helped me at the time to think about other children enjoying the stories I'd read to my babies.

There was a short phase where I had the girls' friends over to pick out things to remember them by. They responded in a million different ways. Some hugged me tightly and burst with joy, others hid behind their mothers, scared my curse was contagious. I've watched a few of them continue into adulthood, while others I've lost track of, and some I can't remember at all anymore.

Amara's best friend, Jade, has stayed in my orbit. Over the years, she'd come to our holiday parties. She'd grow up to be the go-to babysitter, as well as the savior of a forlorn family member. See, when shit went down on July 10, 2012, there was another survivor that needed rescuing—our cat, Opal.

Besides Blake, Opal was the only witness to the events that day. Although I loved her, I was in no shape to keep her with me, so the police handed her to Jade and the two became inseparable.

Months later, when Matt welcomed me to cohabitate with him and offered to add Opal to his cadre of creatures, I considered it, but in my heart I knew Jade needed Opal and Opal needed her. Fast-forward seven years later. Opal was ensconced in Jade's dorm room, with the required documentation certifying Opal's admission to college as an emotional support animal.

Once all of the belongings were out of the house, the keys were handed over to Blake's parents and they tried to sell it. I can't fathom why they didn't just let it go into foreclosure. Blake's mom, Darcy, got a local realtor to list it.

At first, I thought it was ridiculous—who'd ever want to live in the same rooms where three little girls had bled out? Once I accepted it was very possible for the crime scene to be sold, and potentially for a profit, I stopped laughing and began to worry.

My fear was it would sell and Blake would no longer qualify for a public defender, derailing the trial. I tried to call the realtor directly to plea my case, but couldn't get through. I wasn't her client so she really couldn't talk to me about it directly anyway. But then I put my fears up on Facebook and the community responded, to say the least, quite strongly.

The pressure of their social media wrath convinced her that any commission she'd make off the house where the murder of little kids happened wasn't worth her reputation. Quickly, she dropped the listing, and the house never sold. Blake never got a dime. Eventually, the house would be demolished.

I watched the footage from my new home—an old neighbor had texted me video she took. It was surreal watching the big machines crash into the sides of the house, toppling it in a matter of minutes. Several years later, a new home was erected in its place. The address is different and the house looks nothing like the one I still wander in my dreams.

The first time I went back to visit I had no reason to be there other than I needed to finally face the place where my girls had died. I was on my way to a retreat up north where I intended to write this book. Before going to the highway, I made a quick detour and indulged in a drive-by with a brief tap on my brakes to catch my breath.

Gone were the rooms that sheltered my loves in their last moments. My heart ached anew to think of all the laughter and shrieking that once bounced off of those walls. There would be a big empty lot where the girls once ran, and played, and grew. The stop sign Sophie would climb and perch on top of was still there, but that was all. Even the mailbox was gone.

With the house out of the way, my parents and I took refuge in the safe harbor of Sam's abode for several weeks. After that, I rented a two-bedroom apartment for about a minute, mostly just a cover. I think I slept there one night. Most mornings I'd wake up in Matthew's bed to the kind, wet eyes of Solomon, his white Labrador.

I wasn't a dog person then, but a cat lady through and through. It's not that I didn't like dogs, it was just that I had such little experience with them. Solomon taught me why dogs were made to be such clichés. He was an old man when we met and with an elder's patience, he knew what I needed.

Matt would often go to work early, before I was conscious, and so I'd emerge from dreams of my daughters or nightmares of their murderer all alone in the house. At first, the reality would hit me like a punch. Every morning. Amara, Sophie, and Cecilia were dead. I wasn't anyone's mother anymore. It hurt so badly to just exist. Then I'd hear this snort—or maybe snuffle is a better description—this subtle, insistent sound that made me turn my face from the abyss to the other side of the bed. And there Solomon would be, his head resting on the bed staring at me. When my eyes finally locked onto his, his tail would start to wag.

"Time to get up and get on with it," he'd convey through some witchy dog telepathy. "Enough moping. I gotta pee and you should really pet me for a bit."

There was only once he had to bark to get my ass out of bed. Once I was up and moving, I was able to keep going. It only occurred to me much later that he was used to being alone all day, that he wasn't the one in the house who actually needed taking care of.

The last week of September, my parents returned to Illinois. Their lives had also come to a screeching halt July 10, 2012 and it was time for them to go home and pick up what pieces they could. When the world fell apart, we clung to each other until the smoke cleared and we could each find our way back to the lives we had left behind in the rubble.

I had been burned to ashes by the losses of Amara, Sophie, and Cecilia and now the seed of my soul was growing anew. That is a process that will never end. I was in therapy, rebuilding my heart, and facing new adventures internally and globally. When I came back from a healing journey in Asia, I broke my lease to move in with Matt. I still used a P.O. Box, but I finally had all of my shoes, books, and heirlooms in one place.

Matt and I spent a year trying to make the starter home he bought with his first wife ours, but it didn't work. The walls had seen too much of his past, and frankly the kitchen was too small to accommodate the dinners I dreamed would take place in our future. Before we left, we still managed to make a bit of history within those walls.

In the living room, he got down on one knee and asked me to believe in love again. I said yes without hesitation. Shortly before his knee hit the floor, our daughter Trinity's impending existence was announced to his daughters, Elli and Maya, at the kitchen table. Our family started to come together under that roof, but we knew it couldn't grow there.

In October 2013, after being unmoored for a year and three months, we closed on our new home. I finally had a place that was mine and the space to start over again.

Chapter Fifteen

This Is Me Trying

Time is a strange and capricious character. How much difference a single day can make and how little changes in half a decade is a conundrum I still contemplate. Dates mean nothing until they mean everything. November 16th never mattered to me enough to note its passing. Now, it's a personal holiday of joy and sorrow.

On November 16, 2012, I beheld the bodies of my deceased daughters for the last time. On November 16, 2013, I married my second husband, Matthew.

I know what you're thinking. Why on Earth would someone get married on such a gruesome anniversary? Well, like with a lot of things, I didn't have much of a choice. Obviously, I didn't have a say in the slaughter of my children, but as far as the wedding, our options were stripped from us by the laws of man, the whims of Mother Nature, and admittedly, our own making.

There were the usual restraints we all encounter when trying to pick a date to accommodate the events of life and death—turns out, I'm not the only one who has working hours, ranked responsibilities, and suffers the limitations of physical laws. I couldn't mandate Matt's custody schedule or violate Wisconsin's rules about how soon after a divorce someone can remarry. And anyway, grieving three children tends to fill a calendar up with anniversaries of hard days, leaving few easy days to choose from.

To be honest, I didn't even make the connection until a few years ago. I didn't recall the connection when I was sprinkling some of their ashes on my bouquet. It did not occur to me that the same couples who stood by as I laid my hands on Amara's, Sophie's, and Cecilia's flesh for the final time were holding me up a year later as I pledged my tattered heart and soul to Matthew. I didn't forget what I'd been through, and I wasn't being flippant about what I was embarking on, I was just living in the moment and letting the days blur by.

I only found out after Facebook implemented their "memories" feature. I happened to click on the feature, and saw my post for November 16, 2012.

> *Today, I am going to see my girls for the first time since I said a hurried stressed out good-bye to them at the dentist office the morning of July 10th, then I am going to go with them to say a final farewell before they are cremated. I am honestly terrified but know this is what I need to do. Very much like the days they were, this day is going to be horrifically painful and yet hopefully end with some peace.*

Then came the section for November 16, 2013—filled with pictures from our wedding.

That's right, Facebook pointed out to me that I'd chosen to get married on the same date I'd cremated my dearly departed daughters.

Okay, let's back up a little bit here.

Shortly after their murders, I was offered the opportunity to view the girls. I was told their bodies were no longer the products of my womb, as they were now property of the legal system, and so I should not anticipate being able to reclaim what remained of them until after the trial was over. But, if I wanted to, I could look at them.

The medical examiner for St. Croix County came to the hotel I was being sheltered in. She was gentle and honest. She let me know if I chose to view them, it was something I could never unsee, unfeel, or undo. The fog of trauma had cleared enough during her visit for me to see the horizon of my strength, and I knew I wasn't capable of holding my babies' bodies before giving them back to be frozen for months. I suspected the sight of their autopsied remains would drive me completely insane. So, I let that opportunity slip by and carried on carrying on.

I had accepted that the process of burying my children would be lengthy and convoluted. Average mourners get walloped with it all at once. First, take in that the part of your heart that walks around beating outside of your body has stopped. Then, view what's left of your most cherished people. Next, memorialize the short lives that didn't leave near enough scraps to be stitched into a large enough bandage to cover the oozing wound in your core. And finally, entomb, burn, or bury what needs to be enshrined, then leave a marker for the rest of the world to see.

I went through all those steps, plus several extra hoops that only the victims of murder get to jump through. I just had to do it all out of order and it dragged out over a year.

After they told me the girls were gone, I stopped being a person for large stretches of time and turned into just a sound. Just like Black Francis wailed in "Hey" from the Pixies, it's damn near impossible to do anything when you are nothing but pain. Luckily, I had people to do all the things I couldn't.

The biggest hurdle came up almost immediately after the girls were discovered. Their bodies still had to be identified.

One day, the police had come to the hotel conference room we were using as our base of operations—or familial insane asylum, depending on the moment—and asked my parents if they would do the honors. Someone else shielded them and took the bullet instead.

My brother Jack, who hadn't spoken to me in three years after the great Christmas debacle of 2008, dropped his grudge the instant he found out my world had ended. He flew to my side and stepped back into his big brother shoes, for which I'll always be grateful. I appreciated being able to lean on him in those days, and will never forget it. Ultimately, it was him and Quinn who'd hold the scars from identifying the girls even to this day.

Quinn told me later that they were taken to a room where police laid out headshots one at a time. They held it together for Amara and Sophie, but Baby Cea had been especially brutalized.

For a long time, I had egotistically believed Blake had hurt Cecilia more than the others because she looked exactly like me. But I gave him too much humanity, and myself too much credit for that level of influence. I understand now that her injuries had little to do with the emotions a psychopath lacks and more an experiment in physical capabilities.

I believe he was trying to see if he could kill without bloodshed and evidence, so he tried strangling the littlest one first. When he found that he couldn't efficiently throttle her, he moved onto Plan B—slicing their throats. This is probably why Amara and Sophie died instantly and almost painlessly.

I remember when I was told how the girls were killed. We were in the hotel conference room and the family gathered around as the person—who, to this day, is little more than a smudge in my memory—told us the official cause of death was blood loss from having their tiny throats cut with an unknown sharp object. My father Rhett, who'd survived the front lines of Vietnam, was destroyed by those few words.

It looked like a heart attack.

He was sitting in a chair gripping the armrests, his face a stoic mask of determination. But as the words coalesced into an undeniable truth, my father's face crumpled and his entire body began to shake. He curled around the pain and simply fell apart, gasping for air. When the ambulance arrived and the EMT began examining him for his invisible injuries, I thought Blake was going to succeed in robbing me of my father in addition to my children.

Once the crisis passed, my dad was able to get some medicine to buffer the blows, and I think it was officially declared a panic attack. Nonetheless, those days aged him decades.

They never officially found and identified the murder weapon, but I know in my gut Blake used a box cutter. He once bragged that with his carpenter's knowledge he could use one to cut through an entire house. What is a body but a home for a soul?

The second time I was told how the girls were slaughtered was a few months later. The prosecuting attorneys wanted me to know the details before I stumbled across them, so I went to their offices for a late night meeting. Initially, I was going to just run over by myself—grief can make you dumb as well as numb—but they insisted I not drive myself, so I guilt-tripped Matt into taking me.

Matthew had been my ever-enduring rock, my knight in shining armor, the ballast in my emotional ship. He'd already taken on so much traumatic baggage in the course of our still-fresh relationship that I'd just assumed his emotional locker was bottomless. Everyone has their limits, and this meeting turned out to be the first wall that his tank of empathy couldn't barrel through.

The meeting ended and the grisly knowledge of Cecilia's suffering followed us out. I could feel the anger emanating and the defenses rising as we walked out to the car. The first couple of miles slid past in silence. I kept my eyes trained on the horizon.

"Are we ok?" I whispered. "Is something wrong? You seem really upset."

Matthew took a deep breath. "I can't get the image of her out of my head," he said through gritted teeth. "I don't want to know what happened to her. I know enough. I didn't need to hear that. I just can't take anymore. Why did you make me come with you?"

We had only known each other for about nine months at this point. I was terrified that he was going to shut down on me and push me away.

"I'm so sorry," I said softly. "They told me to bring someone to help me get through this and I couldn't think of anyone else to hold me together. I wish I could erase everything you just heard. I'm sorry, so sorry that I have brought this pain into your life."

"It's not your fault," he said. "It just hurts so much more than I thought it could."

Assistant District Attorney Amber Hahn and Assistant Wisconsin Attorney General Gary Freyberg were as gentle as they could be with us, but there is no way to honestly describe what happened to Cea without damaging the listener.

I don't blame Matt for being angry at me for making him know things that no one should ever have to deal with in their lifetime. It wasn't really me he was angry at, and we were able to work past it quickly. I blame Blake for not only destroying those beautiful girls, but for leaving a slew of damaged men in his wake. More than one police officer retired after the girls' murders, and many more of the professionals who had to deal with the case were traumatized by the things they witnessed. These big tough men and women who protect us, love us, and do the hard jobs that keep our families and societies running couldn't bear the sight of my broken babies.

So, this is me warning you that what I am about to describe is Cea's haunting end. What Blake did is impossible to unknow and so horrible that many do not want it shared. This is my baby's truth, and it can't be softened. There is no softening the slaughter of children. Please don't take this as a dare. You can know that she suffered more than her sisters without having to carry the gory details away with you. The book was designed to make it easy to skip this part and there is no shame in doing so.

Warning: Graphic Details

Blake began by strangling Cea until she lost consciousness. When it became obvious to him that he wasn't able to quickly and efficiently snuff her out that way, he cut her throat. He did a shit job of it, though, because according to the forensic evidence found, she died face down on the floor with both of her itty-bitty hands wrapped around her throat trying to hold her blood in.

Years later, when I spoke to the coroner who performed the autopsies, he calmly told me that Amara and Sophie both died before they even realized what was happening. Their father had cut both carotid arteries and death was almost instantaneous.

When I tried to ask about Cecilia, he broke down and refused to say anymore beyond saying she had suffered.

When Sophie was alive and younger, she went through a phase where she called every bad guy "a robber." I tried to explain that bad people do lots of things, not just thieving. But after she left me behind in the most permanent way, I realized she was right. Villains do rob their victims of the most precious things—life, time, and love.

Back to the business of dealing with the bodies. Or, not dealing with them as the case may have been.

I spent most of the four months that the girls were in the freezer not dealing with much beyond surviving. I spent a whole month of that time on the other side of the world.

My college roommate, Misty, had a beautiful wedding in Chicago. I immersed myself in denial and pretended the girls were visiting family as the plan had been before they died. I even followed through with being one of Misty's bridesmaids. Nobody cared when I broke down sobbing occasionally, or followed the sobbing with hysterical laughing, and they most certainly didn't comment on my drunken dancing. Matt came with, and fate saw that I caught the bouquet and he snatched the garter.

Misty and her partner, Nyles, had been there for the immediate aftermath and stayed through the memorial service, so they knew what kind of train wreck to expect. But they accepted me anyway. I can't remember when exactly the idea came up, but at some point, they turned to each other and said, "You know what would really make our honeymoon the best ever? If we brought a recently bereaved and horribly traumatized mother with us!"

I'd spent my twenties birthing people not globe-trotting, or even really state-trotting. I was thirty-three years old when I got my first passport. And the first time I left the continent, I went to China and India for a month. If you're gonna go, go big!

Nyles's family is mostly in China, so my adventure wasn't your typical touristy trip—I had handlers moving me from place to place. Being in a foreign world lessened the blow of my losses just enough to let my heart heal a little so I could start using some of the coping skills my therapist was giving me. Grief does not stop at the border and it's not the kind of baggage you can check, but seeing how large the world is and how universal love is helps.

Standing in the middle of the Taj Mahal showed me just how massive love can be, and how long it can endure. Climbing the stairs of the Great Wall gave me a perspective of how ancient human suffering is, and that all obstacles can be overcome. Participating in the Ganga Aarti ceremony on the Ganges River in Varanasi helped me understand that I could mourn my girls every day and that I'll never be alone in celebrating the lives of loves lost. That trip may have saved my life. It most certainly taught me many of the lessons I needed to find the strength to live on.

I had just gotten back into the country when I received a gutting call. I was jet-lagged and working out with a friend at one of those open-all-the-time fitness places, still trying to process how I managed to technically arrive home timewise before I left China, an aspect of world travel that still blows my mind. I was fumbling off the treadmill when my phone rang and my mother's voice filled my ears.

"Everyone told me to give you time to get adjusted before telling you this, but I can't wait any longer," she nearly shouted.

"Ma, I'm in a public place," I said. "Should it wait until I am some place more private?"

She blurted it out instead. "They've released the girls' bodies."

"What does that mean? I don't understand," I said. "They said we wouldn't get them until the trial was over. What happened?"

But before she responded, I knew I had to hang up. I mumbled something and ended the call.

I had spent so much energy accepting that I'd have to wait and wait to see the girls again that I wasn't prepared for the emotional whiplash this news created. Yet again, I was faced with making a lot of choices I simply wasn't capable of making. Luckily, Bakken-Young Funeral Home—owned by Jodie Bakken-Young and her husband Brian Young—would help carry me through it.

They took possession of the bodies from the State of Wisconsin, worked what magic they could to make them presentable, then arranged for a chosen few of us to say farewell.

Grieving can be such an individual process while mourning is often a communal event, so it's no surprise that often conflict arrives. "Your grief is stepping on the toes of my mourning! My sorrow needs this seat in the front pew! Please take your denial to the cry room in the back? This space is reserved for those in the depression stage, thanks!" And the biggest conflicts tend to arise amongst those of us who shared the same fiery blood.

One of the first big points of friction arose while planning the viewing. Amara, Sophie, and Cea needed clothes to wear since the little cardboard coffins wouldn't cover the top halves of their bodies. My parents very much wanted to participate in picking out special clothes for them, and I was happy to have them help as I've never been much of a shopper. Jodie, however, was delicately blunt with me—the girls needed clothes that would cover their mutilated necks.

I told my parents this even more subtly, assuming that self-preservation would kick in and they'd buy appropriate clothes. The first round of dresses were beautiful and very much what the girls would have loved, but they also would have exposed the wounds from their murders and scars from their autopsies. Luckily, we had a solution.

My mother, Louise, had been a phenomenal knitter for decades. Her creations have adorned our bodies, blanketed us through deep winters, and even held our gifts from Santa. So after the first round of garment choices were shot down, she offered to knit scarves. The scarves were gorgeous, but unfortunately, sheer lacey things. Excellent accessories, but awful concealers. I finally had to face the depth of my mother's denial and hammer home the fact that the girls had to wear turtlenecks.

"But they hated turtlenecks!" she wailed desperately.

"I know, Mom, but he cut their throats and I do not want to have to see that," I said. "If you can't do it, I'll find some myself. They can wear the scarves over the turtlenecks."

My mother and a friend searched high and low but couldn't find any turtleneck shirts. Around this time, I attended a birthday party for Matthew's niece and nephew. Lo and behold, three gifts in, the kids unwrapped turtleneck shirts for themselves. So, of course, I proceeded to royally lose my shit.

I ran from the room and hid in the basement, weeping hysterically and trying to tear my hair out to turn my emotional frustration into physical pain. Matt's sister found me and calmed me down. His mother Johanna, who'd given her living, breathing grandchildren the triggering shirts offered to buy the turtlenecks for the girls viewing. So, when I finally laid eyes on my daughters after four long months, their cadavers were attired in turtlenecks with lacey knitted scarves on top.

The viewing was a very small affair, open only to our most inner circle who I felt could benefit from saying good-bye in body and soul. For the life of me, I can't remember who all was there nor who I'd invited. Matthew virtually carried me through the whole journey from his car into the funeral home and past their corpses.

Before we left the confines of his car, he insisted on praying. He is a man of deep faith, and it is that faith that's led him to stay with me despite the horrors.

He prayed for strength, understanding, and the girls. But me? I'm not much of a praying person. I've never requested much from the universe, instead just trying to be in a place of gratitude for what I did have. I hold firm to the idea that if I'm not praying in the good times, I don't get to pray during the hard times. It's not that I think it's wrong to pray, it's just not my way.

We sat in the parking lot and walked our separate spiritual paths to the same sorrowful summit. While he prayed, I gathered my energy and focused on the moment at hand. I pictured in my mind the invisible strings that connect me to my girls, and the ones that connect us all to the universe.

And then we got out of the car to see my girls.

I remember the moment I walked into the basement where the cadavers were lined up—oldest to youngest, head to toe, with a little space between.

My first thought was simply, "Oh."

That hollow thought filled my being for eons until the next moment came with the bone deep knowledge that they were gone. Their souls were not in those carcasses. Those bodies were just empty shells.

I examined their faces and hands and hair—every inch that wasn't covered—and there was nothing left of what made them *them*. Their hair was ashen. Their faces muted. I could see from across the room that they'd become inanimate objects. They were searched and searched but nary a trace of Amara, Sophie, and Cecilia Lee was left.

Matthew had never met the girls, and I was compelled to make him understand that these piles of cells laid out before us were not my loves.

"They really were so much more beautiful than this," I said softly.

"I know, honey," he said as he held me up. "I know."

Jodie had told me to refrain from trying to hug or pick them up. Turns out corpses that have been cut up and put back together a few times can fall apart in the arms of deranged mothers. Luckily, I didn't have any of those urges. I was content to gently touch and kiss the few areas of exposed skin that remained.

Their souls weren't the only things missing. Amara wasn't wearing her trademark glasses, nor the earrings she was so proud of. Sophie's hands were clean of marker and paint stains. And someone had forgotten to affix a smile to Cecilia's face.

Final touches were laid upon little hands and last kisses were left on closed eyes. Then the girls were loaded up and sent to the crematorium. I don't recall how we got there or how it was decided who'd see the girls' bodies burned.

My memory picks up in a velvet-clad waiting room. The room was tiny and packed with six solemn adults. Quinn and her husband Brian, Megan and her girlfriend Bela, and Matt and I were just taking up space, waiting to be told what to do next. The tension was terrible, and so I made a trademark terrible joke.

"Seriously guys, the next time we do a triple-date, let's think of something less depressing, eh?"

They couldn't help but chuckle.

We were led into the oven room. The crematorium had to fire up an older oven they rarely used in order to accommodate all three girls simultaneously. As it did, I said good-bye to each of my daughters one last time before watching the cardboard coffins roll into the waiting furnaces. The doors were closed, and I stood there transfixed.

"I can almost hear Amara asking a million questions," I blurted out. "'How hot does it get in there? At what temperature will my bones burn?' And Sophie making a joke about me ruining her chances of being a zombie someday."

I broke down in tears when I couldn't even imagine what Cecilia would think of all this—I hadn't gotten enough time with her. Really, I hadn't gotten enough time with any of them.

After all that, they were mixed together and divided into three piles— one in a rosemaled urn for me to keep, one in a plain urn to bury, and one divided into little bags to be doled out to family and friends.

I still have no recollection of leaving that room, and I know a part of me is still in there. The rest of me, however, continued to travel through the days and months following November 16, 2012 until the Earth made one full trip around the sun.

That morning, I woke up in the Old Rittenhouse Inn in Bayfield, Wisconsin. Matthew and I wanted a small intimate affair to commemorate our nuptials.

We kept things as simple as possible. We found a minister willing to officiate our joining despite having different beliefs. Close friends provided music, photography, and other duties. Yet again, I was fairly pregnant while walking down the aisle, but this time there was no pomp or circumstance to cover it up. Matt wore tweed while I had a flowy dress the color of dusty roses. We both wore blue shoes and walked each other down the aisle.

I missed the girls so much that day. I'd sprinkled some of their ashes on my bouquet of "ditch weeds" as I called the wildflowers the florist had put together for me. This was the first of many big events I'd have to get through with them in my heart but not by my side.

Matthew and I stood in front of those who'd stood with us through so much pain and trauma to watch as we declared our love and devotion to each other.

"I love your strength, your kindness," he started, then added, "and your boobs."

Elli and Maya, Matthew's daughters, were horrified but the rest of the congregants just laughed along with us.

After bearing so much darkness for so long, it felt good to feed the light.

Chapter Sixteen

The Field

I was so blind before I lost the girls.

I was aware in a peripheral way of the women and men who had lost their babies and children to accidents, disease, stillbirth, and violence, but I was ignorant of how many people were walking around with child-sized holes in their arms. It wasn't until I was placed firmly in their ranks that I grasped how much camaraderie I had in my suffering. I wish I was alone on this path, and no one else would ever have to carry this pain. I'd be lying if I didn't admit that on some days, knowing I wasn't the only one suffering made it possible to carry on.

I was in recently-bereaved parents boot camp, Halos of Hudson, an organization centered on miscarriage, stillbirth, and infant loss, which was a great support. They gave me necklaces in honor of my babies, and shared their stories of loss and survival. When we had the burial service in May of 2013 to bury a third of the girls' ashes at the headstone, the Halos stepped up again. They commissioned a jeweler to create an intricate necklace with a dash of ashes sealed into the center. It's a solid heart within a hollow heart, and I often joke that it looks a little like a uterus.

For a while it seemed every time I turned around there was another broken-hearted, strong-willed woman lending me her strength.

There was one mom named Dierdre who had lost her two young children in a very similar way—her husband killed them, then committed suicide. After she saw my story, she came to the memorial and introduced herself. We met up a couple months later to share our unique grief and some wine.

Another time, I was out running with a group of women when one slowed her pace to match my strides. She told me of the day her husband accidentally backed over their toddler while leaving for work. She told me the pain is always there but becomes more bearable as the years slip by. She then spoke of the dangers of guilt and how it can destroy love, but also how it, in its own way, feeds love and helps it grow. We ran side by side, our heart rates increasing until talking was no longer an option. I let her words sink in.

I decided that this was how I'd survive. One step at a time. One memory at a time. I'd breath in pain and exhale love. Every moment I'd carry Amara, Sophie, and Cecilia with me, and no matter how heavy the grief would become I'd never leave them behind.

That didn't mean I was without moments of petty jealousy during this whole process. I remember one shameful time when I was reading a Facebook post by a mother who'd just lost her child to cancer. *At least she got to say good-bye!* I seethed internally. *She got to be there with her baby when they died. I bet she didn't have to wait for their bodies!*

It quickly dawned on me, however, that although those things were true, it wasn't the full reality. That mother had to spend months, maybe even longer, watching her child suffer. She had to sit by while they were slowly taken away from her, cell by cell. It doesn't matter how it's dished out, it all hurts. We all have our trials to face.

Meanwhile, as I was putting these pieces back together, I was prepping for the biggest trial of my life.

Legal machines move slowly yet insistently. The first part of the process is the investigation and evidence gathering, and for that I was interviewed a couple times, maybe more.

My computer and phone were digitally autopsied and put back together again. Detectives traveled from North Dakota to central Illinois and everywhere in between to interview witnesses. The prosecutors, police departments, and victim advocates worked diligently to build a case and find justice for my girls. My home was searched and searched again, to such an extent that even after the house was released so we could re-enter, more evidence was found.

It was on the second or maybe third day after we were allowed back into the house when my family found Amara's blood-spattered glasses in her room.

My future brother-in-law, Calvin, was helping to pack up items from the girls' rooms. They each had a blanket and a lovey (aka a stuffed animal loved until it's stuffing was falling out) that they absolutely could not live without, and now that they were dead, I was desperate to cling to those items. Amara had a stuffed elephant named Elli and a blanket that, after over a decade of daily use, was little more than tattered scraps of fabric. While searching Amara's bedroom for these treasures, Calvin found her trademark glasses under the bed. He called the police and had them pick them up for evidence.

I also heard later that at some point in the investigation, police determined one of Blake's last fatherly acts was putting each child against the wall in the kitchen where we'd tracked their growth and measured them one last time. So, before the trial began, investigators removed that chunk of wall to put the entire thing on display in the hearings.

All the while, the defense team was also doing their job. They attempted to interview me more than once. The first time I told them to respectfully fuck off—just because I wanted him to have an adequate defense didn't mean I wanted to help. The second time, the public defender walked up to Matthew's house and left a handwritten letter that tried to bait me by suggesting he had answers to all of my lingering questions. As if spending a few hours with that lying psychopath would give them any insight.

I was heartbroken and devastated, but I knew even then that I'd never in this world get the real answers to the questions I had. I wanted to know if the girls knew how much I loved them in those last moments. I wanted to know what their last words were. I wanted to know where they were now, and if they were together. And some questions, like why and how—physically, how was it possible for him to do it—simply do not have answers.

Evil is an explanation, not an answer.

So, instead of falling for it, I got my own attorney. He wrote up a lengthy letter in lawyerly parlance that essentially told them to fuck off, and vaguely threatened legal actions if they didn't.

I stopped reading the news for more than a year after the girls died. I didn't just avoid stories about my family, I boycotted them all, wrapping myself up in a blanket of ignorance, getting my information in edited tidbits from friends and family. So, when it came time for the trial, I took that method and applied it there as well.

While I participated as minimally as possible—I did have to testify for my babies, and had to be there for the verdict and the sentencing—I did not have to listen to strangers, friends, and family as they testified. If Blake had deigned to speak, I would not have shown up to hear what he had to say. None of it was going to bring the girls back. I just needed him to be held responsible and caged for life.

My family made it possible for me to indulge in this ignorance. My Uncle Stone, as my designated representative, became the shield between me and the public from the first days after the murders until the last appeal failed in court. As the defendant, he was present every day of the trial.

Several of my family members devoured every article and watched every minute of the trial. They would gently prod me to see how much I wanted to know. It turns out, very little.

However, I did learn some things via osmosis, and these facts still haunt me.

One is that Blake had tried to hire people to kill us all. He had kept offering to pay some of his co-workers to kill us, but nobody reported it at the time because it was usually when he'd been drinking and no one took him seriously. He'd also told his cousin that he was more homicidal than suicidal, but again, it wasn't taken seriously. Yet, even after all of this, he still had loyalists willing to defend him.

One was Peyton, my old friend and the woman who I'd trusted to care for my children when I returned to work in 2009. During the days leading up to the trial she'd contacted me to let me know that she'd be a witness for the defense. I thought she was confused about the legal system and felt guilt about her being labeled as such.

"Oh, don't worry about that," I told her. "Technically, I'm a witness for the defense, too. They get to call all the witnesses first, it's just the process."

She quickly burst my bubble.

"No. I am testifying for him," she said. "I am going to defend him."

I couldn't process how someone who had genuinely loved my children and had no familial obligations to their killer could do that. The only explanation that made sense to me is that Blake had an affair of some kind with her. Prior to this confession of loyalty to him, I wouldn't have thought it was even a possibility.

It had started as a business relationship—I paid her to care for Amara, Sophie, and Cea while I worked—but our families had been intertwined for several years. Peyton had also been a social worker until her twins were born, and her husband was a construction worker like Blake. Her twins were the same age as Cea, and were her first BFFs that she had sleepovers with. When Amara read the first Harry Potter book, Peyton was the one who sewed her an invisibility cloak as a reward. Dewayne, Peyton's husband, was one of Blake's few friends, and we often socialized as couples or families. Later, when Blake and I separated, I lost them as friends. At the time I'd assumed it was because Dewayne was the one maintaining the connection, but Peyton's decision to testify on his behalf showed me I was wrong.

Halfway through our conversation, I hung up the phone and then blocked her in every way I could. Later, I found out she'd been visiting

Blake regularly in jail. There are very few people that I simply can't handle being around and she's one, but it's a small town, and crossing paths is inevitable. One time I was invited to a housewarming party by an old church friend. I showed up with Matt, his kids, and an armful of food to share. We walked in the door, I saw Peyton, and turned on a dime. I had everyone back in the car and driving away before the screen door swung shut.

The second of Blake's loyalists was a man named Rufus. He'd worked with Blake in Minot, North Dakota but I never met the man. I remember when we were separating that he had this new work friend he was helping out, so maybe that was him. That is one of the hard things I had to accept about Blake. He could be generous and kind, and that elicited loyalty from those he gave attention to. He wasn't a hundred percent evil all the time.

According to a newspaper article I later read, Rufus called a psychiatric nurse line prior to heading into the courthouse to testify. He made some vague threats to harm the prosecutors and other witnesses, and so the nurse called dispatch and Rufus was met at the door by deputies. They searched him and found a couple of knives. Another knife was later found in his truck. Rufus was arrested and charged. Eventually, he was convicted.

The Victim Advocate informed us of the incident before the newspapers ran the story, and Matt was so unnerved by the threats that he implemented additional safety measures at home. He replaced every lock with a deadbolt and purchased a gun. It is terrifying to be the focus of someone so unhinged and delusional.

Fortunately, there was a little comedy to balance it out. Like when I got wind of the defense's obscure theory to get Blake off the hook.

I was still avoiding any real direct consumption of the trial, but was living with and surrounded by people who were diligently watching every minute. I overheard my mother and sister talking about how the state had paid thousands of dollars to fly an expert in from California to diagnose Blake with Catathymic Homicide. Essentially, the forensic psychologist tried to say that Blake had been dependent first on his mom, and then transferred that dependence to me. To end his dependence, he had to murder the kids.

When I found this out, I burst out laughing. Honestly, I was relieved this was the best they could come up with, some convoluted mommy issues.

I did have some moments of fear and doubt that he'd be let off, though. Who wouldn't think that what he'd done was completely insane? I dug deep and held tight to the faith that he'd be seen for the evil man he was, and that the jury would realize he was too dangerous to ever be released into our world again.

I have since found the courage to read some of the articles on the trial, and in doing so, I know that I made the right choice. I could have easily obsessed over every detail—watching every YouTube clip of testimony, poisoning myself with trollish comments left by anonymous haters—but I do think this information blackout was pivotal in my long-term recovery. I was so vulnerable those first months after the girls died, I didn't need to know the cruel details of how badly I failed to protect them. I couldn't hurt anymore than I already did.

I remember only a few moments of my testimony, and was even shocked later when I read I was questioned for two whole days. Most clearly, I remember all the people who came to watch and give me strength. So much love, so much kindness, so much courage. I still regret not being strong enough to have been there when my friends and family took the stand, but they knew I was sending as much energy as I could spare from behind closed doors.

My biggest concern initially was controlling myself in close proximity with the murderer of my children.

Plus, there were detailed meetings with the prosecution, victim advocates, and court bailiffs on who would be placed where as I made my way to the witness stand.

At first, I thought they were concerned for my safety, but I guess my desire to tear Blake apart with my bare hands was showing a bit more than I knew. Even now, I only remember the minister holding me back in the jail that first night after I heard Blake on the other side of a door, but they all recall that it actually took *three* people, including a trained police officer, to restrain me.

I guess all that exercise had made me pretty strong. Oops.

As I walked past the defense table on my way to the stand I repeated a mantra to myself. *Death is a mercy he does not deserve. Death is a mercy he does not deserve.*

Over and over, I repeated this in my mind until I found myself seated in the box and ready to honor my girls as best I could. Calm, cool, collected are all great descriptions of other witnesses, but not me.

"Are these your daughters?" was the first question from the prosecution, while indicating a large picture of Amara, Sophie, and Cecilia.

I answered with a sob. "Yes, those are my babies," I said.

I was always going to do what I had to for Amara, Sophie, and Cecilia. I knew every day of the previous nine months that I would take the stand for them. Standing up before the court to ensure my daughters got justice was never in question. How much of the time I spent crying was anyone's guess. The rest of the questions and answers are a complete smudge in my memory except for two moments.

Blake's attorney asked me something I found to be completely nonsensical, something along the lines of, was there anything about Blake that had been the same since the beginning of our relationship?

"Well," I replied, "he has been consistently tall since I first met him."

Laughter rippled through the jury and the crowd. It even echoed from the defendant. I looked right at him and just thought, *No, you do not get to laugh at my jokes anymore.* The glimmer of the laughter we'd shared over the years almost broke my resolve to not mutilate him there on the spot.

The only other moment I remember clearly was between Prosecutor Amber Hahn and myself. I think the defense had tried to build a case that, because I was a licensed professional in social work, my name-calling was the equivalent of a legitimate mental health diagnosis. We had to go through this charade, despite the fact that I was not an MD or PhD or any of the D's that are the only ones who can legally diagnose an illness. Amber needed to have it in the record exactly what I had called Blake, and on more than one occasion.

The defense was attempting to get into evidence that I had called Blake "insane" to help support their argument that he was legally insane, but Amber made sure that the entirety of my insults were entered into the record. I never left it at a simple statement about his sanity but always added in a few choice words to let him know just what I thought of him.

So when Amber asked me on the stand exactly what I said, I leaned into the microphone and stated, "I called him an insane douche bag."

My time in the witness box came to an end and the trial continued on without me. Evidence was entered, theories were debated, and more witnesses were called to testify. I didn't return to the courthouse until the final day for closing arguments, and then to await the verdict.

So many people came together to carry my family through this trial, it was simply amazing. There was love and positive energy pouring in from across the country. I was so thankful for it, but I was only one woman and could not absorb it all.

I also wasn't ready to let Amara, Sophie, and Cecilia's story end with a criminal case. I wanted the world to think about how they lived, not how they died. I wanted their murderer's crimes to be overshadowed by their happy memories. How could I possibly make that happen?

A group of us were gathered in a room somewhere in the bowels of the county courthouse awaiting the verdict. People came and went, but I stayed put—after all, this was where the food that local restaurants had donated was being doled out. My parents were there, along with other friends and relatives. Hannah Bellrichard and Samantha Jensen were amongst the throng.

Hannah was the daughter of Pam, our primary Victim Advocate, and Sam was not just her best friend, but had also volunteered in Sophie's classroom. Sam and Hannah were wrapping up their senior years at River Falls High School. It was a small town.

Someone had floated the idea of a memorial around the room. My mother had a friend who had a friend who was in the playground business of sorts. Unlimited Play was a company that did fundraising for and coordinated the building of handicap-accessible playgrounds around the country. All of their playgrounds were in honor of a local child with disabilities. This resonated with me as the perfect opportunity to use the energy created by the girls' deaths to make something as beautiful and as playful as they had been.

I didn't want just a cold statue or impermanent plant to remember them by; I needed something living and active that would create new memories. Others were looking for a way to keep the momentum of positivity going as well, and Sam and Hannah leapt up and caught this butterfly fragile idea in their net of enthusiasm.

That was on April 16th, and by July 20th those two amazing teenagers would be overseeing a 5K run attended by thousands raising $50,000 for the Tri-Angels Playground.

I'd like to say I poured my whole self into the project, but that would be complete bullshit. At best, I redirected all of the goodwill and love away from myself and into this project. I was still recovering from the trauma of losing my precious girls. I simply didn't have it in me to commit the time and energy it would take to build a committee and raise the money to build my dream.

Fortunately, there was an army of saints and citizens rearing to go. I would show up at events as my slow recovery allowed and used every media opportunity I could to raise awareness about the playground. The true builders and workers and fundraisers have their names etched on slides and listed on signs around the playground for all to see.

The playground would never have been built without these amazing people busting their asses to make the world a better place! But that was a future I couldn't even imagine yet in that courtroom.

As we sat for hours waiting for twelve jurors to come to a consensus about whether or not Blake was responsible for his heinous crimes, I held equal amounts of faith and fear in my heart. I was terrified they'd find him insane and he would be released to stalk me once again. If he was sent to a mental institution instead of a prison, I would never be safe, and neither would anyone I cared about. I tried to keep the anxiety at bay by focusing on the nugget of faith I had in my fellow humans. They needed to see past his posturing and lies and give my girls the justice they deserved. As the minutes ticked by and there still wasn't a verdict, I found it harder and harder to imagine a future where I could heal. It became harder and harder to breathe as I continued to wait.

Finally, we were called back into the courtroom. I sat between my future husband and my mother on a hard bench, and survived the slow minutes by scrolling through pictures of the girls on my phone as we waited. The jury filed in and filled the box.

I searched for signs of what they had decided in their body language but found nothing concrete. I don't know what I was hoping for, a thumbs up? The judge entered and my vision tunneled until I saw nothing but my hands in my lap.

My hands that had held Amara, Sophie, and Cecilia. My hands that had made their meals, smoothed their hair, and wiped away their tears. I missed them so much and would have given anything to touch them once more.

When the jury declared that, yes, Blake was a twisted piece of shit and completely responsible for his actions, I was flooded by a relief so deep my lungs seemed to fill for the first time in months.

He was guilty. He was going to prison and would never breathe free air again.

The courtroom exploded with noise of…not exactly joy, because there is nothing joyful about justice for murdered children, but of righteous consolation. There were sobs of relief mixed with guttural cries.

I exalted in the end of a trial of tribulations only to turn around and face the abyss of lifelong grief. I wasn't the only one to be slammed by a tsunami of a thousand emotions at once.

More time would be spent in that courtroom for the sentencing and the inevitable appeals, but in that moment, I felt like I had finished an emotional marathon. Now that I knew I would be safe from Blake's wrath, hope began to grow in my heart that I could carry on.

Chapter Seventeen

You Were Born

04/23/14

Dear Trinity Hope,

Salutations, my love!

I am sure if you're reading this, you may have some questions regarding your name, your existence, and your purpose. Or maybe you don't care two bits about any of all that and just get a kick out of reading my rambling writings.

By now, you certainly have some knowledge about your mama and should know that one of the core components of my personality is honesty. I will be painfully, bluntly, and consistently truthful with you. So, some of this will be hard to take in, but that's just how life is.

Let's start with why you're here.

You exist because your three sisters were murdered by their father. You exist because I needed you to be able to carry on in this world. You exist because I still believe in love. You were not conceived on a whim.

When I lost your sisters, I lost my purpose and identity. My first response to the idea of having another child was, How could I possibly bring another child into such a horrible world? How could I subject a child to growing up with such a ghastly legacy tied to them? Obviously, the universe has deemed me unfit to be a mother, and who am I to argue with that judgment?

I thought long and hard about these questions. I thought about them day and night, drunk and sober. I thought about them in the depths of my grief, in the heights of my enlightenment. Then, I stopped thinking and faced the knowledge that if I were to remain a part of this world, I needed to live it as a mother.

I chose the path of love and hope, and embraced my selfish need to live for someone else.

I considered adoption, but soon realized that it wasn't a realistic option due to my own internal issues and systematic barriers. Our family, to some extent, is built on adoption. Your great grandfather was adopted, as is my youngest cousin. I fantasized about adopting a trio of orphaned children and our broken hearts melding together over time, but as a social worker I knew that the reality would never live up to my dream. You see, adoption agencies would take one glance at my trauma history and politely decline my applications. I had to be honest about my own bone-deep fears. I knew I could not handle the risks that accompany adoption. The possibility that a biological parent or family could come out of the woodwork one day and take my children away was too much to bear.

The next option, then, was to make a baby. But that too was more complicated than it sounds. I'd gotten my tubes tied the year before because, well, I was done having babies! I had three daughters and was a single mom working full-time. When I made the decision to go through with another pregnancy, I met with my doctor who explained my options.

I could do IVF—who knew they could still harvest your eggs even if your tubes are tied? —or they could reconnect my tubes. IVF would have been very expensive, but almost 100% guaranteed to work due to my age and fertility. On the other hand, having my tubes fixed gave me a 70% chance of success. The doctor and hospital offered to donate the cost of the reversal surgery to me, an enormously generous gift.

I chose this latter route because I liked the idea of a higher power still being involved.

If it was meant to be, it would be.

But, Trinity, the final piece of this particular puzzle was important. That's who you call dad.

I did fleetingly consider using an anonymous donor and artificial insemination to truly have a child that was all mine and nobody else's. Your dad was going through a lot himself at the time, and asking him to jump on the baby bandwagon with me was frightening. I wanted to give you the best possible family, and that included a loving, present, and involved father.

I was blessed to have your dad come into my life at just the right time. He had a lot of concerns about his future and how having a baby with me would affect Elliana and Maya, his existing daughters, your half-sisters. He put aside his fears, put his faith in God, and joined me to bring a wonderful new soul into the world.

Timing is everything, they say. I knew getting through the second year without the girls would be far harder than the first. The first year I had shock and denial to cushion me, obligations and trials to distract me. The second year all I had was acceptance and grief. I did not want to wait too long but wanted to wait long enough. So we did.

We waited until Amara, Sophie, and Cecilia could be buried. We waited until their murderer was found guilty and sent to jail for the rest of his life. We waited to make sure we could blend the family that was and the family to come. We waited until the time was as right as it could be, and then we made you.

Your father had a first name picked out before you were the size of a lentil bean. Matthew was a man of deep faith when I met him, and he relied on that faith to guide him and support him as he cared for me. He wanted to name you for the three core aspects of that Christian faith—the trinity of the Father, the Son, and the Holy Spirit.

I embraced your name for other reasons. "Trinity" is a memorial to the three sisters that you won't be able to meet in this life, but since we knew you would grow up in the shadow of their deaths, we wanted to acknowledge it right out in front with your name. I wanted the name to be a talisman, giving you the power to not let the past define you. Maybe it will help you claim ownership of the tragedy, versus it looming over your life.

I came up with "Hope" as your middle name to remind you that you were conceived out of just that, and not out of sorrow. Existence is often hard, painful, and unpredictable. Life is often easy, joyful, and trustworthy. Hope is the key to surviving the difficult so we can luxuriate in the idyllic.

People are brought into this world for all sorts of reasons, and often for no reasons at all. You were born with a shadow of tragedy behind you and a beacon of love to guide you. You were not born to replace anyone, you were not born to balance a great injustice, you were not born to be my salvation.

You, my love, were born to be you!

With the best of intentions,

Mama

"You were born into a strange world.
Like a candle, you were meant to share the fire.
I don't know where we come from, and I don't know where we go.
But my arms were made to hold you, so I will never let you go.
Cuz you were born to change this life.
You were born to chase the light.
You were born…"

Cloud Cult, "You Were Born"

Chapter Eighteen

Only Son of the Ladiesman

After I lost Amara, Sophie, and Cecilia, gifts of all shapes and sizes flooded in.

They came from friends and strangers, clergy and bikers, artists and doctors, shipping in from near and far. I don't even know how some of them found me considering my own nomadic ramblings those first three months. Some gifts made national news and others will only ever be known by me. Even to this day, trinkets still appear by their headstone with no indication from whence they came.

My family's tragedy predated GoFundMe by about a minute or two, but still, the first gift to come pouring in was cash. Lots and lots of cash.

Vincent Depaul, a businessman from Hudson, Wisconsin with a panache for groundroots fundraising, set up a chair in a parking lot and spread the word that he was collecting money for my family. Thousands upon thousands of dollars came in, and soon an official fund was set up at a local River Falls bank. Vincent later coordinated with other businesses in town to provide meals for my family during the trial. Once, after I'd been drowning my sorrow in liquor at one of his fine establishments, he even drove me home.

Those first few weeks, when I was grasping to hold onto reality with both hands, I did not have a free one to fully hold the enormity of the fundraising. All I could think was, "What use is money, what use is anything now?" Well, I can tell you now that the money absolutely made my recovery possible.

It paid for therapy (*so, so much therapy*), shelter, a healing trip to Asia, a bottle or ten of liquid courage, the preservation and display of the girls' artwork that I'd saved, and much more. That money was used to help start the fundraising for the playground, and later, I was able to make my own donations to other families struggling with their own traumas.

Not all the gifts I received were currency, though. There were stuffed animals, signed soccer balls, engraved jewelry, and many works of art, both garish and precious.

I also received a plethora of books. Some were stories trying to prove that there is life after death, others were blueprints from every religion for how to carry on with grief. There were heartfelt tales from other parents who were also left bereft, and empty journals for me to fill in with my own writings. All these books helped me in small ways and through hard moments, but the one that's carried me the furthest simply appeared one day shortly after the girls had died.

It was ensconced in a manila envelope with no return address and randomly added to a pile of correspondence that had poured in from all over the country. Inside was a book wrapped in hot pink fake leather with flowers embossed all over it. I knew as soon as I read the inscription I'd carry it with me for the rest of my days.

The first page was filled with this handwritten note:

Mother,

Stay alive in some way, shape or form. Your beautiful girls are rooting for you, not wanting you to be so sad. Do not fear because we all are mortal ourselves. Find peace, find rhythm, find calmness. Read a page a day, then when you are done, read it again. Read it for the next years of your life so that you can tell your girls all that you have learned when you are reunited with them. Stay alive so that I can stay alive before meeting my own son, too. Up in paradise, we are all families, who only know of love and good energy.

~Another Mother

The rest of the book was filled in with various hand-picked poems, lyrics, and quotes for the mourning soul. It's been with me to the ends of the world, physically and spiritually. Even the poem that I had engraved on my babies' headstone came from this book.

Whoever you are, dear book-maker, please know that you may have saved my life.

Another book given to me in the early days was *Keep Going: The Art of Perseverance* by Joseph M. Marshall, III. The writings of those who had also experienced loss gave me hope for recovery. Even if I couldn't see my own path through at the time, I had evidence that such a journey was possible. Over the years, it's become my go-to volume for giving to others in the throes of grief.

The greatest gifts, by far, have come from my own body. Namely, a couple of complicated creations that tie me up with their invisible strings.

One day in 2011, I was rushing to Target to buy a few things I needed and several things that I had no intention of getting—the curse of shopping—when I walked through the doors and immediately beheld my possible future. There was a woman about my age cradling her newborn while fighting with her teenage daughter and ignoring two younger kids making laps around the cart.

Hell no! I thought. *I have had it with pregnancies!*

I swear my uterus attempted to flee my body in that moment. I went home and called my doctor right away to have my tubes tied.

Fast forward to early 2013, after everything had changed, and I was being rolled back into surgery where tiny robots would stitch my tubes back together to give me a fighting chance of making a new life.

My OB, who'd delivered Cecilia and been the one to cut my tubes in the first place, had made all the arrangements. He volunteered his skills and worked with the hospital to donate their portion of the surgery. After the robots were done, I had slightly better than a 50/50 chance of regaining the mantle of mother.

My body may have been ready, but I wasn't mentally yet. I still had to get through the trial, making sure that myself and those I love would be safe from the terrorist who could still weasel his way into a mental health ward instead of a prison. So I waited, made sure he was convicted of his crimes and stripped of his freedom, then had the final funeral service for the girls, the last step being the internment of some of their ashes under their headstone.

Then, being completely bare and vulnerable here, I needed time to take suicide off my list of back-up plans.

When the universe failed to strike me dead as it goddamn should have, I accepted that I was going to have to carry on a bit longer. I had work to do. Justice to secure, children to bury, affairs to get in order. I was also very motivated to not add to the awful grief that my friends and family were already carrying.

More days than not, I'd find myself longing to be run over by a garbage truck. I'd stand on a street corner staring at two tons of metal and think, "It'd be really nice if it would just keep coming." Inevitably, it would turn the corner. Eventually, so did I.

The closest I came to the edge of self-inflicted oblivion was June of 2013. I just had to get through the sentencing hearing, then all my work was done, making my ties to the future tenuous at best. The years and decades of loss and sorrow loomed large. Each of my daughters had already missed birthdays, first days of school, and all the holidays in between. I had spent my first Mother's Day in over a decade childless. I was maudlin and full of rage.

I thought I would start at the house. I would cut my wrists and walk the same path I'd taken a thousand times to the headstone. Once there, I'd curl up on their grave and never have to be without them again.

Anyway, it sounded much more graceful than crawling into a bottle until my liver gave out.

I called my friend Iris. I let her know that I felt like I might be done, done with all this horror and pain. She didn't guilt me or plead with me.

"You could. That's your option," she said. "But I don't think it's what you really want to happen. I don't think it's how you really want to leave."

Then, she trusted me to make the right choice.

The crucible of loss and trauma was breaking me. The relief of ultimate oblivion beckoned to me daily. I wanted out, dammit! I'd had enough of this horror, the pain was too heavy. I could not carry it another moment!

But it had to be carried. If I put it down in that most permanent way, it wouldn't dissolve into nothingness. It would simply smother those left in my wake. And whatever was left of my soul wouldn't tolerate me destroying others in order to stop my own suffering.

So that was that. I learned to move forward.

I had spent the one-year anniversary of Amara, Sophie, and baby Cea's murders in a cabin alone with my memories and a speck of hope. Two days before, I'd found out I was pregnant.

We were officially trying, a novel experience for me whose previous pregnancies were all happenstance, so I was watching my body like a cat watches a mouse hole, waiting for a sign something was happening. I pounced on every tiny change I could. My boobs hurt! I felt queasy! I was mildly more emotional than usual!

The waiting was a special blend of boredom and anxiety. Then, I realized my age wasn't the only thing that had advanced since my first pregnancy back in 2000. Tests had gotten a lot more accurate—I didn't even have to wait until I'd missed a period! I took the test as early as possible, about a week before Aunt Flow was scheduled to arrive. The plus sign was faint but definitely present.

We'd done it! We officially had positive affirmation from the universe that a baby was coming our way.

I was flooded by a deep sense of gratitude flecked with guilt. This was my new reality—every good thing was going to have a tinge of sorrow, but it was my duty to embrace joy while also carrying the grief. This was the first time I had to hold the joy of new love while knowing it only existed because I'd lost my first loves.

All of this was going on as the wheels of justice still plodded along.

The sentencing was on Monday July 15th, 2013, one week after I saw the plus sign. Blake had been found guilty and sane back in April, so the purpose of this hearing was for the judge to officially sentence him. The options available were life in prison for each daughter he destroyed with no chance of freedom, or life sentences but with the possibility of parole. It was also at this time when victims could make statements about the impact crimes had wrecked upon their lives.

I wrote a letter to the judge instead of making a statement to the entire court. I did not want to give Blake any more of myself than I had to. He was not going to get to hear my voice crack or see my tears again.

Others spoke for me as I watched from the galley. My brave, beautiful thirteen-year-old niece Anne stood up in the courtroom and poured out her soul before the judge and witnesses. My sister, Olivia, made sure those present remembered that Blake had become a monster, and only a life buried deep within the prison system would provide safety to those he left behind.

Blake did have some supporters come forward to plead for leniency. I let their statements pass over me barely heard, knowing they were borne of a grief only the mothers of monsters know. The only words that penetrated were when one of them dared to offer him my babies' forgiveness. That was *not* hers to offer. Just as I will never know what the girls felt those last moments, none of them will know if that demon will ever be forgiven.

As the statements were delivered, I watched Blake shrink further and further into himself as reality set in. The judge laid out in no uncertain terms that Blake would never be released from prison.

The flood of relief I felt when he was found guilty back in April surged through me again. I knew there would be apathetic appeals to be made and pedantic pleas for little freedoms. The legal machine would go through the motions of grinding those attempts to dust. The door was closing on Blake and there would be nothing more from him. He was being swept into a dark corner, never to be free again.

During the hearing, I agreed to give my first interview with a local TV station. My motives were clear. I wanted to take as much attention away from Blake as I could and redirect it to fundraising for the Tri-Angels Playground. So, there I was sitting in the gallery as the judge delivered his verdict, when I felt a twinge deep in my belly. I chalked it up to the stress of the day, so I went to the bathroom to prepare for the interview. When I was finished and looked down into the toilet, there was blood.

I had miscarried.

Pam came in and rescued me with feminine products I thought I wouldn't need for the next nine months. I put my strong face on, headed across the hall, and smiled for the interview.

After reviewing blood tests later, the doctor let me know that, yes, I had been pregnant, but it hadn't gone past fertilization. I had been blessed with fertility since I was barely out of my teen years and had been a bystander to many of my friends and relatives losing pregnancies. I was aware it was a possibility for me, but I still didn't see it coming. Three positive tests followed by three grueling pregnancies followed by three beautiful babies had led me to believe I was immune to this particular kind of loss.

It cut me, but I was so bloodied by the loss of the girls that I barely felt it at the time. But now, there are moments when I feel the sharp pain of that tiny loss like a paper cut to my heart. When I'm at a doctor appointment and have to state that I had "six pregnancies and five births," or when I'm on a drive and suddenly out of nowhere I become aware of all the ripple effects of that lost pregnancy. No matter how microscopic that loss was, it still had a deep impact on my soul.

It wasn't long after, I was the recipient of another positive pregnancy test. And this one stuck.

Three days shy of my thirty-fifth birthday, I found my arms again weighed down with a beautiful baby girl.

Trinity Hope Peterson came into this world smiling. She was such a peaceful infant that I would call her my Buddha Baby. As the years passed, she'd shed her serenity and embrace her passionate side. I was later told the first atomic bomb was named "Trinity," and trust me, her temper can live up to it.

I would be lying if I tried to deny the glimmers of the girls that I see in her.

She greatly resembles Sophie, so much so that I had to send out trigger warnings before sharing pictures of her after she got her hair cut short. She is incredibly intelligent, often reminding me of Amara. And although she is not a fan of bugs like Cea was, she shares her adoration of babies. But despite the many similarities, she is very much her own person. She is on her unique journey, shaped by sisters she never got to meet.

It was not long after my little bomb came into my life that God brought forth another miracle…or at least that's how the doctors presented it to me.

Just to recap: First, I'd had my tubes cut, then sewn back together, actions that alone dropped my fertility to at best 70%. Second, I had a baby who I was breastfeeding exclusively. (There are women out there who don't need any other birth control but breastfeeding.) Third, I was past the age, in medical terms, called "advanced maternal age," a.k.a. "ancient," a.k.a. "drying up." Fourth, we just had a baby and romance was not commonplace yet. Fifth and finally, I had an IUD in, arguably one of the most effective forms of birth control at 99.99% effective.

When they looked at the ultrasound, the IUD was indeed right where it was supposed to be. But next to it? There was what would become Flint, nestled snugly into my uterus.

What a trip, huh?

My doctor, and two others, reviewed the ultrasound pictures and declared it was an Act of God. After going over all the risks of leaving the IUD in versus taking it out, we pulled it. The act of removing the IUD after an embryo has staked its claim in a uterus will often end the pregnancy, but not Flint.

He wasn't going anywhere.

We told nine-year-old Elli and seven-year-old Maya via specially-made fortune cookies that said, "In spring, you will have another new baby brother or sister," and "You are being promoted to eldest of four." Their response was "Again?" Trinity was blissfully unaware of the growing addition quickly pushing her out of the family's baby spot.

My body greatly protested the fact it was being asked to support so many lives. In my seventh month, I honestly thought I was simply going to fall apart. I developed a hernia as back-to-back pregnancies are not great for a woman's abdomen. I had to have surgery to keep my guts behind my abdominal muscles, which was successful, but scary as hell. And I'll tell you, having someone kick your surgical stitches from inside is a totally different sort of pain.

Ironically, to monitor the baby, they had me do my recovery in the same maternity ward where Trinity had taken her first breaths. The year previous, when Matt and I had welcomed Trinity, a nurse had come into the room to give us the postpartum birth control talk. This policy-enforced little chat was something all three of us mocked at the time. I mean, come on, we weren't inexperienced in how these things happen. Well, I'll tell you what, when that same nurse strolled in while I was going into labor again, I practically yelled at her, "I had an IUD in! I swear, I listened to you!"

She just chuckled, shook her head.

"Best laid plans…" she said.

Flint was due on the 4th of July, but he decided he didn't want to share his birthday with the country.

I'd been feeling uncomfortable and decided I would come home and lay on the couch instead of trying to work through the rest of a dull Tuesday. I flipped through Netflix's selections until I landed on *The Blacklist*, which I binged. I paused to take care of Trinity when she came home from daycare, then Matt and I returned to our TV binge as we got her settled for the night. The contractions grew harder and closer together until we decided it was time to call Grandma Johanna—Matt's mom—to stay at the house with Trin while we went to the hospital.

Flint was my fifth and final delivery. I honestly do not remember much, and many of the details have blurred with the previous four. Like the rest, there was blood, cussing, and the glory of another battle won. He came into this world at 4:58 a.m. on the first day of July, and like all those who came before, he changed me just a little bit more. Now, I wasn't just a mother but a little boy's mama, a whole new experience.

Flint, oh my heart, having a baby boy is an experience unlike any other. He too shows shades of his sisters who weren't here to welcome him. Strangely enough, Cecilia, Trinity, and Flint were all born in the same hospital, and all three of them were exactly the same size, to the inch and the ounce. And yet, all three went in totally different directions after the first month.

Trinity is my biggest kid by far. Cecilia was solidly average in size and weight when she passed away. Flint is a smidge bigger than Amara was, but a heavy contender for my smallest child award. He has Cecilia's sweetness and a desire to mother those smaller than him. Flint shares Amara's palate and love of all things edible. He looks exactly like Matthew, so much so that strangers who knew Matt as a child were able to tell who I'd married simply because Flint was his carbon copy. He was not planned but he was definitely needed.

I recently went to a workshop to help hone my writing craft and one of the exercises was to write about a time when you knew "it was over." This is what poured out of my heart for my final baby:

I knew you would be my last baby. I had thought before that I was done making people, then my little people were torn from this world by a monster. I began again. I had Trinity and was pretty sure she was the universe's last blessing for me. Then you, baby boy, defied Mother Nature, Father Time, and Sacred Science in one fell blow. You also broke me physically and your father mentally. You completed us. You spiced up our story and rounded us out. 5th for me, 4th for him, and one and only son for us both. I started my parenting voyage with an oops. It felt right to end with a miracle. We tried to prevent you, but in the end, you, dear Flint, were the answer to unsung prayer. I held you and was undone.

When I tell people that I spent two years pregnant, it really felt like it. Having two babies that close together was challenging and rewarding, often just pure joyous chaos. In 2013, I ran my first 5K, the only 5K I've ever run, and I did it in 28 minutes. Go me! When 2014 rolled around, I found myself pushing Trinity in her stroller for the second 5K. On August 15th, six weeks after Flint graced us with his presence, the Tri-Angels Playground was opened to the public.

What a whirlwind!

At the beginning of the process, I was told to expect fundraising for the playground to take many years. We needed over half a million dollars to build the playground of my dreams. The small communities of western Wisconsin heard that and said, "Hold my beer" and just got it done. It was amazing!

It wasn't a couple of big checks from a handful of major donors, more like a few bucks from everyone within a fifty-mile radius. Checks came in from lemonade and cookie stands run by grade schoolers. Local bars ran meat raffles. There were painting events and comedy shows. Almost every business in town had a donation jar next to the register. My future step-daughters (at the time) set up an art sale in front of the grocery store and raked in $473. Calendars displaying copies of images of the girls' artwork were created and sold. Companies large and small donated time, manpower, and materials to the effort. A donor list would be a book unto itself.

One of the most notable was Affinity Plus Credit Union. They were the bank that ended up owning the house after it was foreclosed. Once Blake's ties to the house and property were severed, the bank approached my family. In the beginning, I wanted it burned to the ground and turned it into a community garden. My father had a much better idea.

Rhett requested the home be dismantled and anything useful donated to Habitat for Humanity. Affinity Plus did just that. When they sold the lot to construct a new house, they gave the proceeds to the playground. And because they just couldn't help themselves, they asked the fundraising committee how much more was needed to get us over the limit. They wrote out another check.

The grand opening, August 15, 2015, was a bittersweet day. I missed Amara, Sophie, and Cecilia so badly. It felt so wrong for them to only be with us in spirit. They would have absolutely conquered every aspect of that playground. I looked around at the people surrounding it and saw so much light and love in the faces of all the children still alive and ready to play.

Cloud Cult played a few songs as an opening ceremony of sorts, and I danced with Trinity. When they were finished with their setlist, Trinity looked up at me with glee before making a B-line for the slides, pure joy in her eyes.

Epilogue

Stubborn Love

"Mama, when are you going to tell us how they died?" Trinity asked for the millionth time.

"Baby not yet," I responded. "Someday when you're both old enough to deal with it."

"Was it a car accident?" Flint piped in. "Or did they get sick?"

"I get what you're trying to do there, little man. This game of elimination is not gonna work," I said. "What happened to them was very rare and not something you have to worry about."

I'd like to say these are the hardest inquiries I've had to deflect, but they were the easiest. When lying is not in your parental toolbox, every answer leads to a minefield of further questions.

For example, one night as I was tucking Flint in, he hit me with this one:

"Mommy, what did the ovens look like?" his serious little voice asked while his hands drew the images from his mind in the air. "What shape were they, and how big?"

"What oven, babe?" I asked.

"The one Amara, Sophie, and Cea were burned up in," he patiently explained. "How big was the door? Because if I was there, I would have busted in and saved them."

You don't realize how barbaric cremation is until you explain it to a five-year-old with an engineer's mind.

"Oh, buddy," I sighed, "let's not think about this right before bed. They were dead long before they were cremated."

The world of Trinity and Flint is littered with ghost memorials of their missing sisters.

The daycare they grew up in was where Cecilia went to, so the staff that loved Cea was the same one that shepherded Trinity and Flint from newborns to preschoolers. There was even a Cloud Cult painting and dedication to the girls hanging in the halls. While I was writing this book, they were attending the same elementary school Amara and Sophie went to, and often play around the memorial by the old entrance: three stones bearing three names that linger in the background of their days.

Even the library isn't safe—it has a memorial with beautiful stained glass windows and the inspirational words of Shel Silverstein etched into three subsequent panels.

On April 4, 2019, I took Trin to school for her kindergarten registration. The last time I had been in those rooms was in 2012 with almost five-year-old Cea. This is the Facebook post I shared that day:

> *Today is a good day! A happy day! A milestone of a day! It's also a hard day. A grieving day. A memorial of a day. Trinity's Kindergarten Registration day!*
>
> *So exciting to get a quick glimpse of her future academic home. So hard to wade through the ghosts of what was and what should have been. I almost kept it together. I almost held both worlds without letting them bleed into each other.*
>
> *Almost.*
>
> *When the dam finally broke a bit, there were so many sympathetic souls to stand with me in the flood of emotions.*

Trinity is so pumped for her journey and helped guide me through with her effervescent personality and her disco ball dress. She asked me to take her picture on Cea's rock. Somehow she knew the layers of this moment and knew just how to tie them all together. I'm sure Greenwood is going to teach her a lot of things next year, but I think she already has empathy covered.

Then, of course, there's the playground.

A big, bright beautiful testament to not just my babies but a community of grievers. Trinity has taken to telling anyone we encounter that it's *her* playground because those are *her* sisters. I gently remind her that it isn't ours, it's everyone's.

"Mom. Why do Amara, Sophie, and Cecilia get a playground?" she loudly asked recently as we were driving past. "Shouldn't everyone who dies get a playground? What makes them so special?"

See: minefields and verbal traps abound.

Their deaths aren't the only mysteries that Trinity and Flint are desperate to solve. Blended families are fascinating, too.

Elli and Maya are their living, breathing sisters that live with us for a week, then their mom for a week. This has been Trinity and Flint's reality since they took their first breaths. You'd think it wouldn't be questioned, but alas, this phenomena is prodded constantly.

"Daddy, why did you divorce your first wife? Do you like her? Why does Elli and Maya have to be gone all the time! They've been gone for years! Why are they so sad when they come back?"

Elli and Maya are excellent big sisters, and as hard as the divorce has been for them, they do love their siblings. There's no halves as far as they're concerned.

Early on, before I was even pregnant with Trinity, Elli made a prophetic declaration on a particularly hard day. She was newly eight at the time and was struggling with the split-custody schedule that day.

"The only good thing that can come from this is if I get a baby brother!" she yelled at me.

It took me a couple years, but I did my best to deliver.

Flint is a lover. He falls in love with almost every girl he meets. For a few years, he was very committed to his friend Charlie from daycare. They adored each other before they could even speak in full sentences. He would talk of the pink castle he was going to build for her and all the babies they would have. Then one day, I took him to the playground and he met another little girl. They ran off playing for a bit and a little later he came back to me with big news.

"Mom, I am in love with her!" he said with deadly seriousness.

"Do you even know her name?" I asked.

He ran off to ask her, and she told him it was Harley, so he instantly said, "Harley, will you marry me?"

She readily agreed.

Later, I teased him by saying I was going to tell Charlie about his transgression.

"Dad has two wives," Flint countered. "So can I."

Checkmate.

Inquisitions over the past are dangerous things in the hands of children. I still have all my scrapbooks from when the girls were alive and I was donating half my money and time toward creating elaborate photo albums that, back then, were going by the hot trend phrase "creative memories." I chose not to remove all the pictures of Blake since I didn't want to sacrifice any images of the girls. So now and then, when Trinity and Flint pull them out and pour over them, they inevitably see images of him with the girls, and the questions start anew.

"Momma, why did you divorce your first husband?" they'd ask. "Why is he a bad man? Where is he?"

"He's gone. Long gone," I said, then quickly follow up with a bribe. "Who wants a snack?"

I think what drove home for me just how complicated their worlds are, was filling out a form for Trinity to get occupational therapy. It was going smoothly until I had to answer this question: What is your child's birth order?

It's complicated, that's what it is!

Well let's see, Trinity is her mother's fourth of five. Her father's third of four. Every other week, she is the oldest of two, and in the off-weeks she is a middle child.

Flint, at least, is the baby all the time.

Nine years later I find myself still here, still vulnerable, still growing, and still loving.

Matt and I celebrated our sixth wedding anniversary pandemic-style with takeout from a local restaurant. I continue to earn my living as a social worker as an Adult Protection Investigator, and I have a long-term goal of being a Victims Advocate one day. My parents have retired to Florida and enjoy Trinity and Flint's antics from afar, except for a couple of times a year when they get to experience their shenanigans in person. My tribe is still populated by many of the same people who helped me raise and bury the girls, but new faces also play pivotal roles in nurturing Trinity and Flint, and keeping me sane.

I've lost some family and friends to grief, unfortunately. The pain that my presence elicits is too deep for some to bear, and I respect that. Each of us has our own journey through grief and loss that we have to walk, and often those paths need to divert.

This life that I've built is complex, but so very beautiful, too. I knew that if I was to survive, I would have to create a world I loved as much as the one I lost. I think about this passage written by an unknown author a lot.

Grief never ends, but it changes.
It is a passage, not a place to stay.
The sense of loss must give way if we are to value
the life that was lived.

There have been times when I worry that somehow my continued existence is a slight against Amara, Sophie, and Cecilia. But my grief has not ended, my pain has not abated. I carry them with me in every action I take. Not a day goes by that I don't share some emotional space with them.

My calendar is riddled with hard anniversaries, missed birthdays, and just average days of longing. There is not a season, month, or day that isn't threaded together with grief. There are days when I wake up and feel like I'm surrounded by strangers, and then I realize I am the stranger, that the loss has made me a stranger even to myself.

Who is this woman that walks around with such gaping wounds? Where are the daughters who defined her and made her whole?

"Should be..." is a wall of fire that I walk through. "Would be..." is a brutal wave that crashes into me, and "could have..." is the pit that swallows me whole.

The year 2019 was littered with missed milestones, especially for Amara. High School graduation, senior pictures, acceptance letters from colleges. I was invited to many events, even attended some. I'm sure they would've set an empty chair out for her at the graduation ceremony if I'd have asked, but I didn't want my loss to overshadow her classmates' accomplishments.

That's just part of the shit sandwich you have to swallow when your children are murdered.

My girls are gone, and there are a million and one things they'll never get to do. I've accepted that and I decided long ago I wouldn't hijack the ceremonies and milestones of their peers with my own sorrow.

But then I remember I am Amara, Sophie, and Cecilia's mother and will be always. I am the woman who holds their memories, their very cells still swim in my blood, and their purposes are exposed in my actions. I am not a stranger, for they would see in me all that they were.

The universe saw fit to give me new people to celebrate in the midst of these hard days. New souls to surround me and help carry me forward.

A while back I was reading a book—I have no idea which—and a section made me think this troubling thought: *Is there any limit to the harm people can do to each other?*

At first, my brain was flooded with images of all the horrors that humankind has wrought upon each other, especially those wrought on me personally. And yet the voice in my head responded to this grim idea with a contrary truth.

There is no limit to the kindness people do, either. The harm is like an ocean deep and unfathomable, and the kindness is like air enveloping and luminous.

I'm often asked if I will ever speak to Blake again, if it would help me to face him and question him. Initially, I left the door open for such an event. Maybe after a couple of decades I'd think about it. Now, I am almost certain I will never communicate with him again. It would be like screaming at a brick wall. Whatever had been human in him died with the girls.

I could easily focus on the hate I feel for the man who murdered my children, but I strive for indifference towards him, as that is the true opposite of love. I can't reach that lofty summit just yet, and instead focus my energy on the love I have for all of my children.

I remember the myriad of kindnesses the world has shown in the face of that one vile act to me and my family. I look at the tragedy that has defined my life and choose to let it make me better, not bitter.

You, dear reader, will have tragedies big and small to face as well, for it is the nature of existence. You also can choose a path of light in the darkness.

I presume one of the many defenses people have for holding tight to their hates so obstinately is because they know once hate is banished, they will be forced to deal with the pain.

Well, sir, I say bring the pain.

Matt and I knew the conversation with Trinity and Flint about their sisters was inevitable much like winter in Wisconsin. You can't avoid it, so you might as well prepare.

We were wary and watchful for two particular developments to occur: the children learning to read and increasing access to the godforsaken Internet.

The kids were both in school before we knew it, being taught to read and think for themselves, and we started getting reports from school that the kids had been trying to question some of the teachers who'd taught the girls before they died.

"Did you know my sisters?" they'd ask. "Do you know what happened to them?"

Matt and I knew it was time to gather our arsenal for the parental battle ahead. We had meetings with the school counselor and psychologist, talked to their teachers, got books like *A Kid's Book About Death* by Taryn Schuelke, and even had an hour-long session with a child therapist. All of it was to try and come up with a plan for how to talk to them about how their sisters were murdered, but most of the resources available were for talking about fresh wounds, not old scars.

We adapted what we could to our own unique situation. We would keep it honest and simple. We would choose our words carefully. He would be my ex-husband, not a father or dad. We would say killed, not murdered. And then our well-laid plans grew into a framework we could improvise from. When we were prepared, we would wait until the time was right.

Matt and I had thought we could put it off until the middle of the summer. That way the kids wouldn't be in school, and we thought it would minimize the chances of them sharing their newfound information with friends. We also figured the fascination with how Amara, Sophie, and Cea died would be at a seasonal peak in the summer due to the anniversary.

I don't know why after raising a cumulative of seven souls we thought we knew anything. We'd forgotten about the age-old outer of secrets and supplier of misinformation: peers.

The final days of Trin's first grade year and Flint's kindergarten experience were a barrage of mini-field trips. One day, Trinity's class was taking a short hike from the school to the Tri-Angels Playground, taking them right past the headstone. Naturally, Trinity wanted to share this special spot with her classmates as they tramped past it. Her curious brethren peppered her with questions, many of which she had no answers for. And when she couldn't satisfy them, it upset her.

Her amazing teacher did her best to quell the interrogation and redirected them on their journey. Later at the playground, an older kid from another class caught wind of the drama and decided to taunt Trinity further.

"If you don't even know how they died, then you aren't really their sister!" the kid said. "I know what happened to them because my dad worked on the playground, but I'm not telling you."

Well, that was it. Our time was up. It was time to tell the kids.

It was a sunny Saturday afternoon in early June when Matt and I gathered our strength and called the littles into the living room. I took a deep breath as I waited for their arrival.

"We are going to have a family meeting," I babbled. "We are going to have a talk. We are going to tell you guys what happened to Amara, Sophie, and Cea. Well, not exactly everything, but some things."

"Wait! I think I want something to hold onto!" Flint blurted out and ran into his bedroom while Matt, Trinity and I waited for him.

He quickly returned, holding a pillow over his heart and most of his face, his eyes just barely peeking over the top of it.

"Alright," he said, "now I'm ready."

Recipes

Tuna Casserole

(Amara's favorite and the first thing she learned to cook solo.)

Ingredients

2 small of 1 large can of tuna drained

1 can cream of mushroom soup

1 can cream of asparagus soup

1.5 cups frozen peas

½ cup parmesan cheese

¾ bag of egg noodles cooked

Muenster cheese slices to cover the top

Directions

In a large casserole dish, mix tuna, soups, peas, and parmesan cheese. Stir in cooked noodles. Top with Muenster cheese and then bake at 350 degrees for 45 minutes or until cheese is browned and casserole is bubbly.

Jess's Tortilla Soup

(I made this for Matt on our second date
and claim it is why he fell in love with me.)

Ingredients

The meat from 1 rotisserie chicken

About a tablespoon of olive oil

1 white onion diced

1 purple onion diced

5 cloves of garlic minced

A mixture of fresh chilies, also minced serrano, jalapeno, bullet, Anaheim,
or habanero

1 can black beans, rinsed

1 can corn, drained

1 can petite diced tomatoes with juice

Spices: a generous amount of cinnamon, nutmeg, cloves, and a couple
shakes ancho chili powder

1 box chicken stock

2 cups orange juice

1 can tomato sauce

½ cup tequila (the cheaper the better) plus more to taste

Chopped up variety of fresh veggies—zucchini, yellow squash, colored
peppers

Chopped cilantro about 1/4 cup

Garnishes:

Tortilla chips (thicker the better)

Sour cream

Slices or cubes of avocado and mango

Directions

Put a little oil in the bottom of a big pot and set the heat to mediumish (like 6 on a 10 scale). Add the onion, garlic, and chilies, stir a bit, and then let things get soft. Add the rest of the ingredients in order, adding the veggies 10 minutes prior to serving, and the cilantro the last minute or two.

Place a layer of tortilla chips in the bottom of a bowl, ladle soup over the chips, garnish with a dollop of sour cream and add the avocado and mango.

Pasta Sauce #42

(A nod to *The Hitchhikers Guide to the Galaxy* and the only way I get veggies into my pickiest eaters.)

Ingredients

2-3 tablespoons butter

1 onion, diced

5 cloves of garlic, sliced

Spices: basil, oregano, thyme, fennel, anise, salt, pepper, and a pinch of crushed red pepper

1 red pepper, chopped

1 can diced tomatoes

About 1/3 cup red wine

A bunch of fresh spinach

1 small can of tomato paste (with herbs preferably)

1/3 cup heavy cream

A good splash or swirl of balsamic vinegar

Any noodle that you like, but I go for the veggie noodles with this one

Parmesan cheese to garnish

Directions

Melt butter over mediumish heat, add in onion, garlic, and spices. Let things get soft and translucent. Add the red pepper, red wine, and can of tomatoes. Put a lid on it and let everything get mushy. Add the spinach, stir and cover till it's totally wilted. Use an immersion blender to puree what is in the pot. Add cream and blend some more, add tomato paste and blend it. Add the vinegar and stir it in. Then, just simmer and stir while the noodles cook. Serve with noodles and cheese on top.

Banana Bread

(Flint's favorite and something I started baking after I lost the girls.
I never baked much before, and this became my go to comfort food
after I lost them.)

Ingredients

1/3 cup of butter melted (I use the leftover part of the butter stick to
grease the pan)

3-4 ripe bananas, smashed to smithereens

1 cup light brown sugar

1 egg beaten

1 teaspoon vanilla

1 shot bourbon or brandy or orange liquor

Spices (I don't measure spices. These are in order of most shakes to just a
pinch.) cinnamon, nutmeg, cloves, and cardamom

1.5 cups of flour + 1 tsp baking soda + a pinch of salt, all mixed up

Directions

In a glass mixing bowl, I melt the butter. Then I add the bananas. I use a
hand mixer to turn them into mush. Add the brown sugar and mix until
blended, then add the egg, followed by vanilla and booze of choice, and
finish with spices. Once everything is incorporated, I add the dry flour
mix, mixing until it is the consistency of kids' slime. Pour it in to a but-
tered 4x8 loaf pan. Bake it at 350 degrees for 1 hour. Let it cool before
cutting or it will just fall apart. Store in a sealed container or plastic baggy
to keep it moist.

Trinity's Borscht

(Trinity is picky, but for some reason loves beets...)

Generally, I make one meal where I roast two chickens and beets. I then make stock out of the chicken carcasses and use the leftover chicken meat and the beets. But that is a bit much for most people.

Ingredients

Homemade chicken stock or two boxes

Chicken from a rotisserie chicken or leftover roasted chicken

Leftover bite size chunks of purple and/or golden beets or peeled and diced beets (just add to stock long enough to boil through)

1 onion, diced

5 cloves of garlic, sliced

1 can petite diced tomatoes

2 large carrots, sliced

Mushrooms, quartered

Spices: bay leaf, paprika (Sweet Hungarian if you can find it), cinnamon, nutmeg, marjoram, salt, pepper, thyme, and some honey

Directions

Put it all in one big pot and cook until veggies are soft. Serve over noodles or with crusty bread. I like sprinkling feta cheese on mine, but nobody else does.

Acknowledgements

Creating this book from the ashes of my soul and binding it with the love that my stubborn heart continues to pump into the world has been an act of healing unlike any other. I would have no book to write without my children Amara, Sophie, Cecilia, Trinity, and Flint who gave me a story worth telling and a reason to keep sharing it. I could not have started nor finished this memoir without the steadfast and loving support of my husband, Matthew Peterson. His belief in me and the power of my story kept me going when self-doubt threatened to derail me. So many of my friends and family encouraged me to speak my truth and let me know that my words could heal wounds and make this world just a little better. If I tried to list them all, the book would be a million pages long. Some souls went above and beyond to give me the tools to bring this memoir into the world of print. Michelle Novak was the engineer building the path for me to follow through the forest of authorship. Through her, I met Rick Paulas, my first editor. Rick challenged me constantly, and often the response in my head would be "FU Rick" but then I would do the work and the results would be epic. Thank you, Rick, for bringing out the best in me despite all my cussing. Michelle continued to be the doula for my memoir by being a first reader and accompanying me to Writers Workshops that Allyson made sure I knew about.

Liz Senoraske and Sally Peterson both kindly provided their homes for me to use for writing retreats. What an amazing gift sacred space is for a writer. Kelly Grenzow also sacrificed some spare time to be a first reader and encouraged me to fight for this book to get into as many hands as possible. Many professional writers were kind enough to encourage me and give me advice on my path to finding a publisher. One such author, Callie Trautmiller, proved that there are no connections quite like small town ones. She kindly introduced me to Brittiany Koren and Written Dreams Publishing, who were brave enough to take on my project. Without their incredible hard work and support, this tome would not be in your hands. Thank you to Ed Vincent for the beautiful cover design.

Then, there is my tribe that has kept me alive and mostly sane over the last decade: Rachel, Carrie, Megan, Sonja, Catherine, Pam, and Tarrah. I would not have had the courage to face the world without you at my back and by my side. My family has been the forge that birthed me, and no matter how fiery it can get, I am thankful to them for making me strong enough to be vulnerable. Thank you Mom, Dad, Mary Liz, and John for your part in making me who I am. Matthew, Elli, Maya, Trinity, and Flint, you have all made it possible for me to put pen to paper over the last five years. You have all sacrificed in small and large ways, and without you, I would have no home. Finally, thank *you* to my readers for reading. My hope is that you can take away something from this story and pass the love on to someone else.

Resources for Grief and Trauma

The Compassionate Friends: https://www.compassionatefriends.org/

Faith's Lodge: https://faithslodge.org/

National Domestic Violence Hotline: https://www.thehotline.org/

The Butterfly Path: https://thebutterflypath.org/

Books I found to be helpful:

Keep Going: The Art of Perseverance by Joseph M. Marshall, III

A Kids Book About Death by Taryn Schuelke

Proof of Heaven: A Neurosurgeon's Journey into the Afterlife by Eben Alexander

About the Author

Jessica Lee Peterson is, first and foremost, a mother who has built her life around raising children. While developing her family, she also pursued a career in social work. She has been a licensed social worker since 2001, helping people and their families navigate complex systems and work through the hardships of life. In July of 2012, Jessica lost her three daughters, Amara, Sophie, and Cecilia to domestic violence. Since then, she has used her grief as fuel to make the world a better place, embracing a philosophy of choosing light over darkness. She works for Washington County as an adult protection investigator and resides in River Falls, Wisconsin with her husband Matthew, stepdaughters Ellianna and Maya, and their children, Trinity and Flint. You can find her on social media at https://twitter.com/Jessica72176596 and https://www.facebook/amarasophiececilia.schaffhausen/ or at her website: thistlesandthorns3x.squarespace.com/home.